MANDALA ORIGAMI

Colour & Create

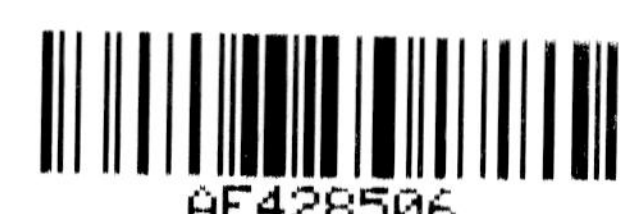

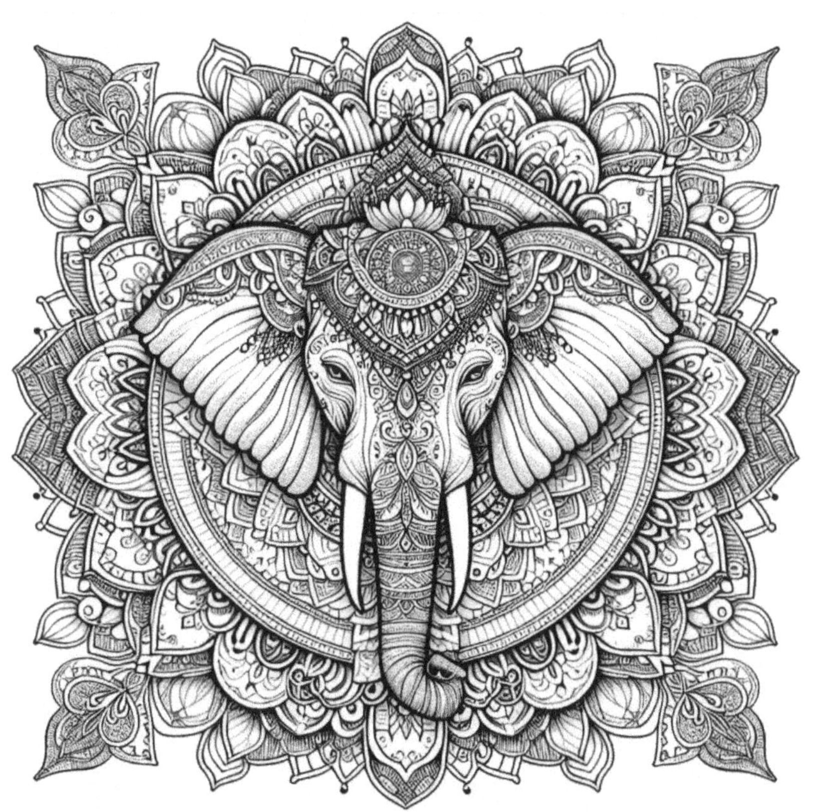

BE CREATIVE

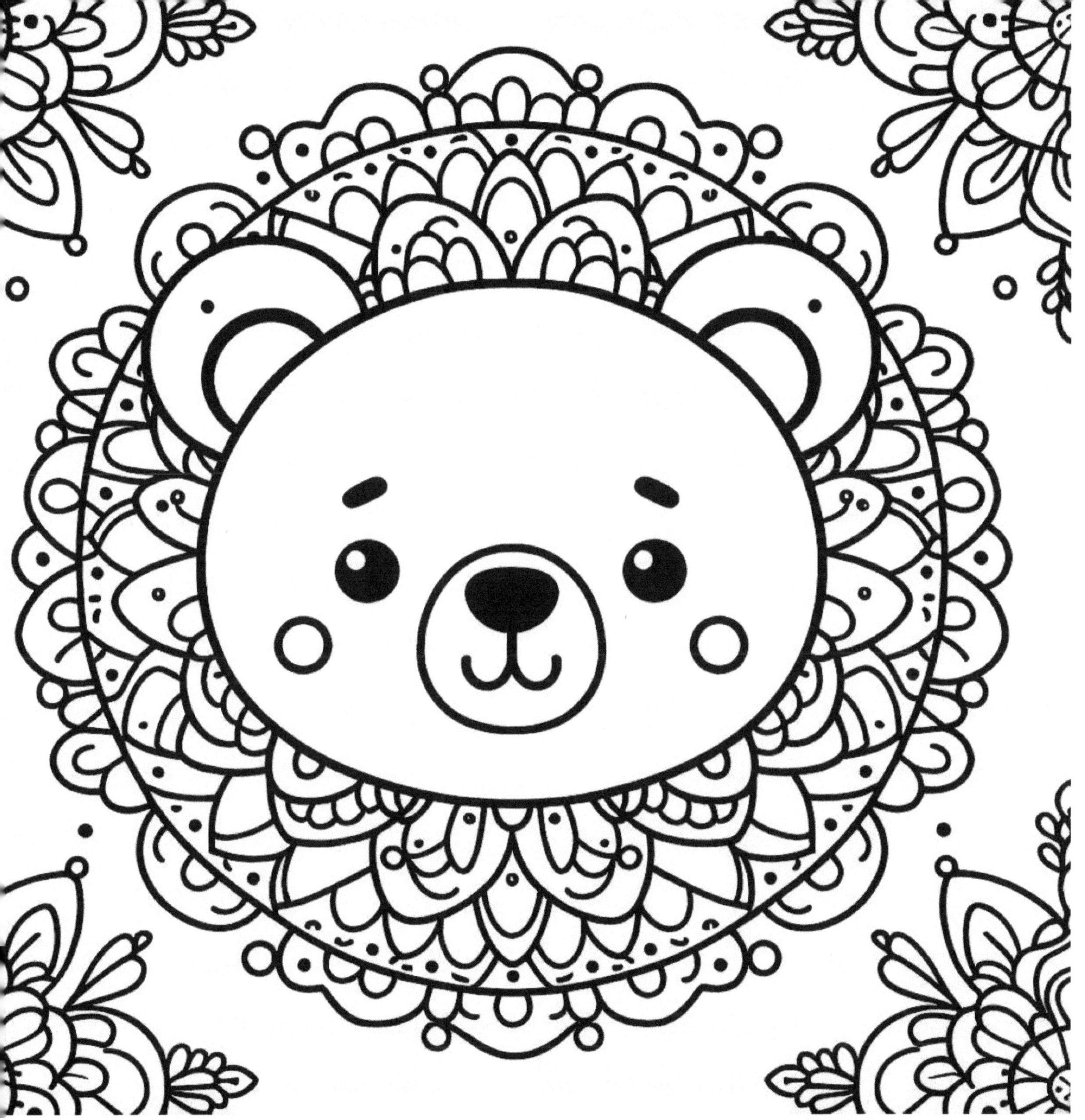

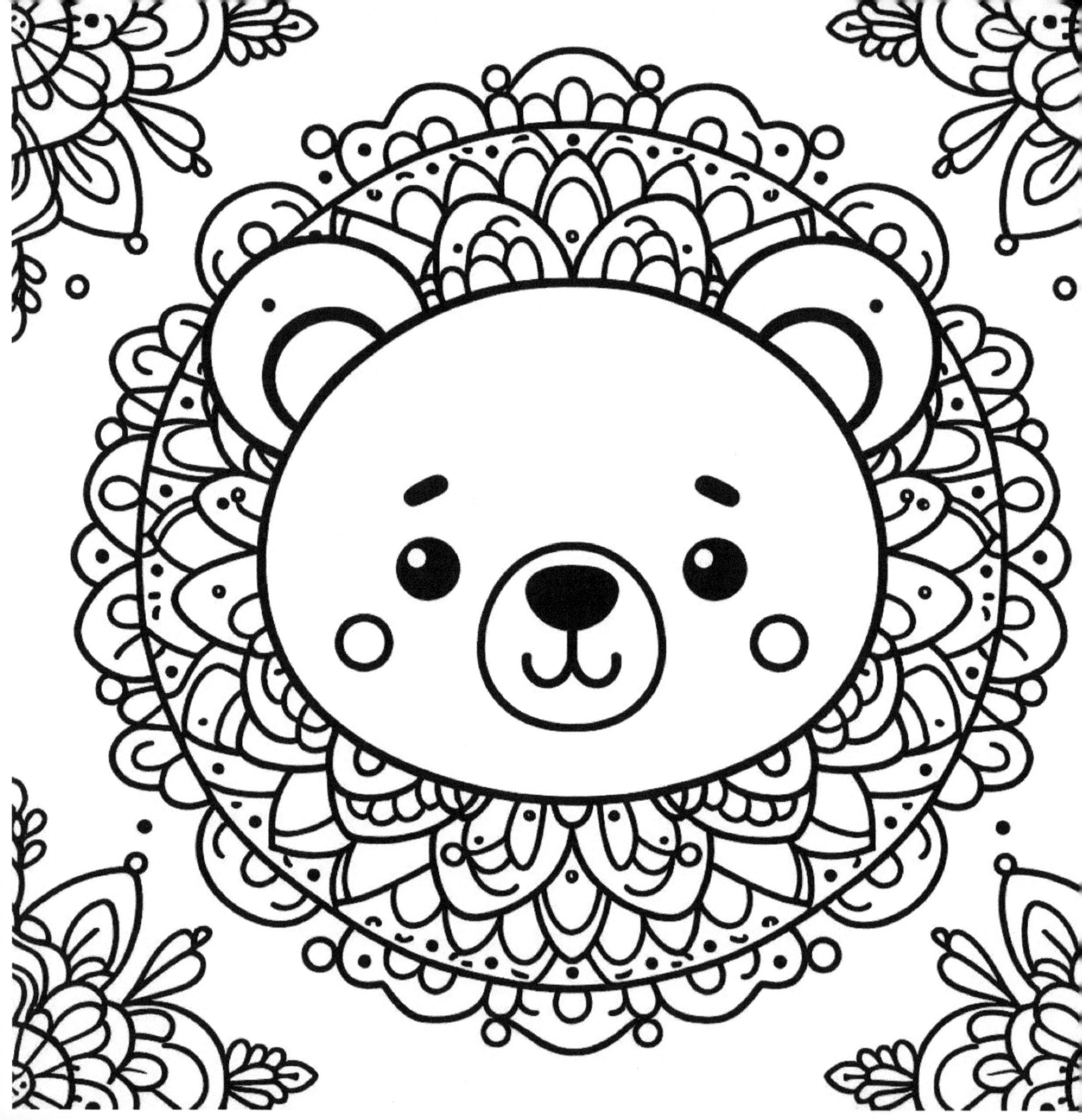

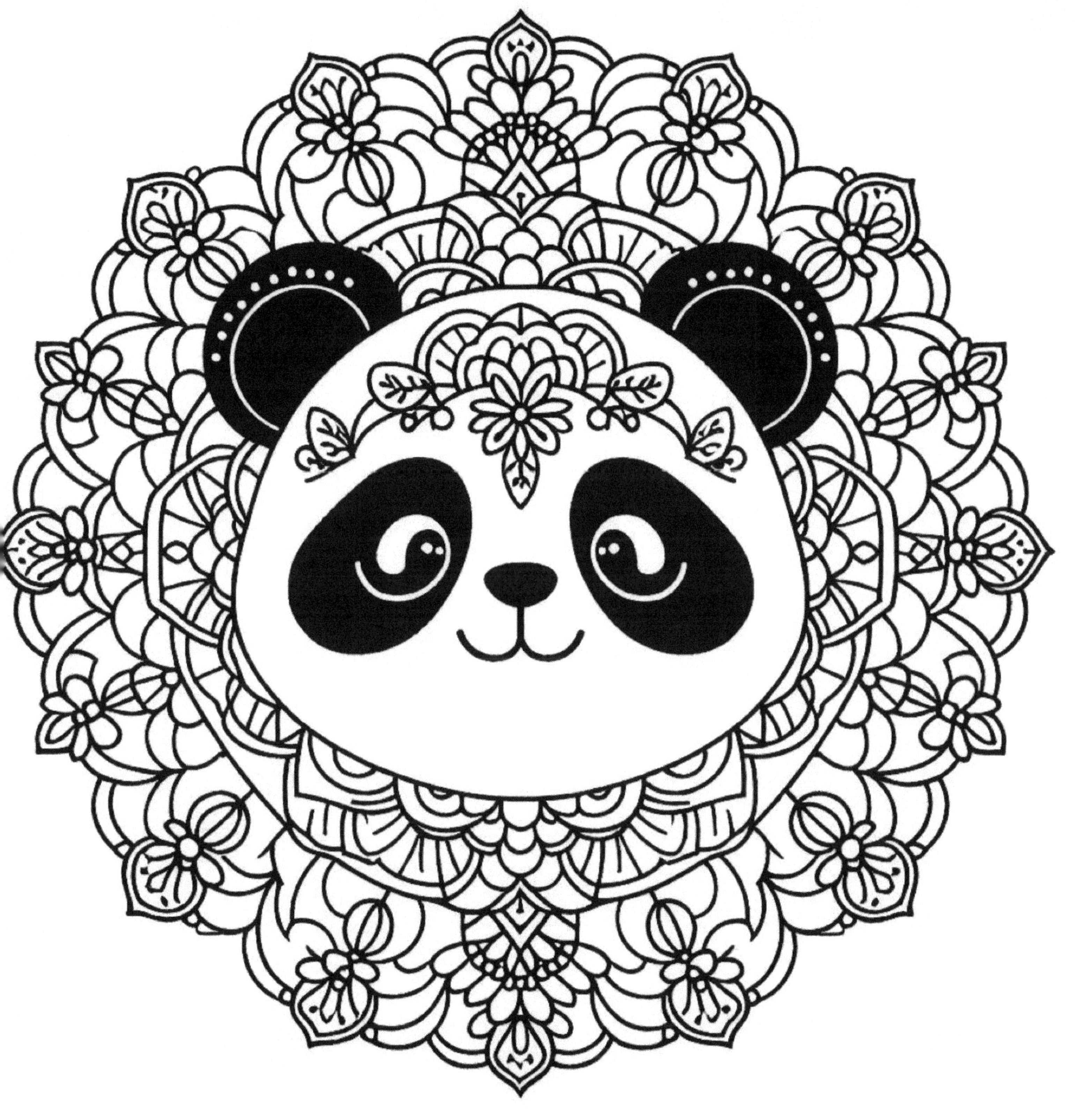

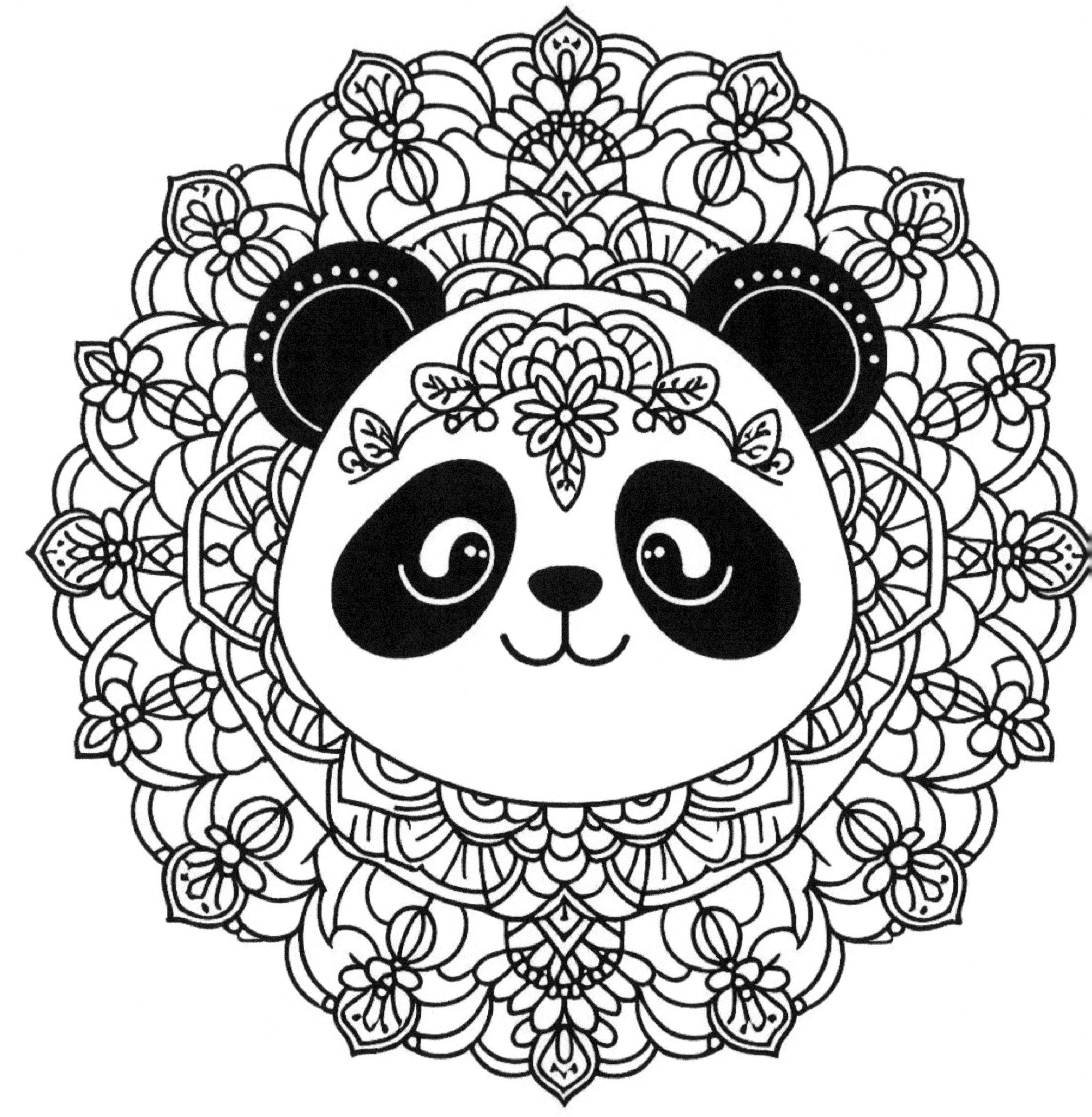

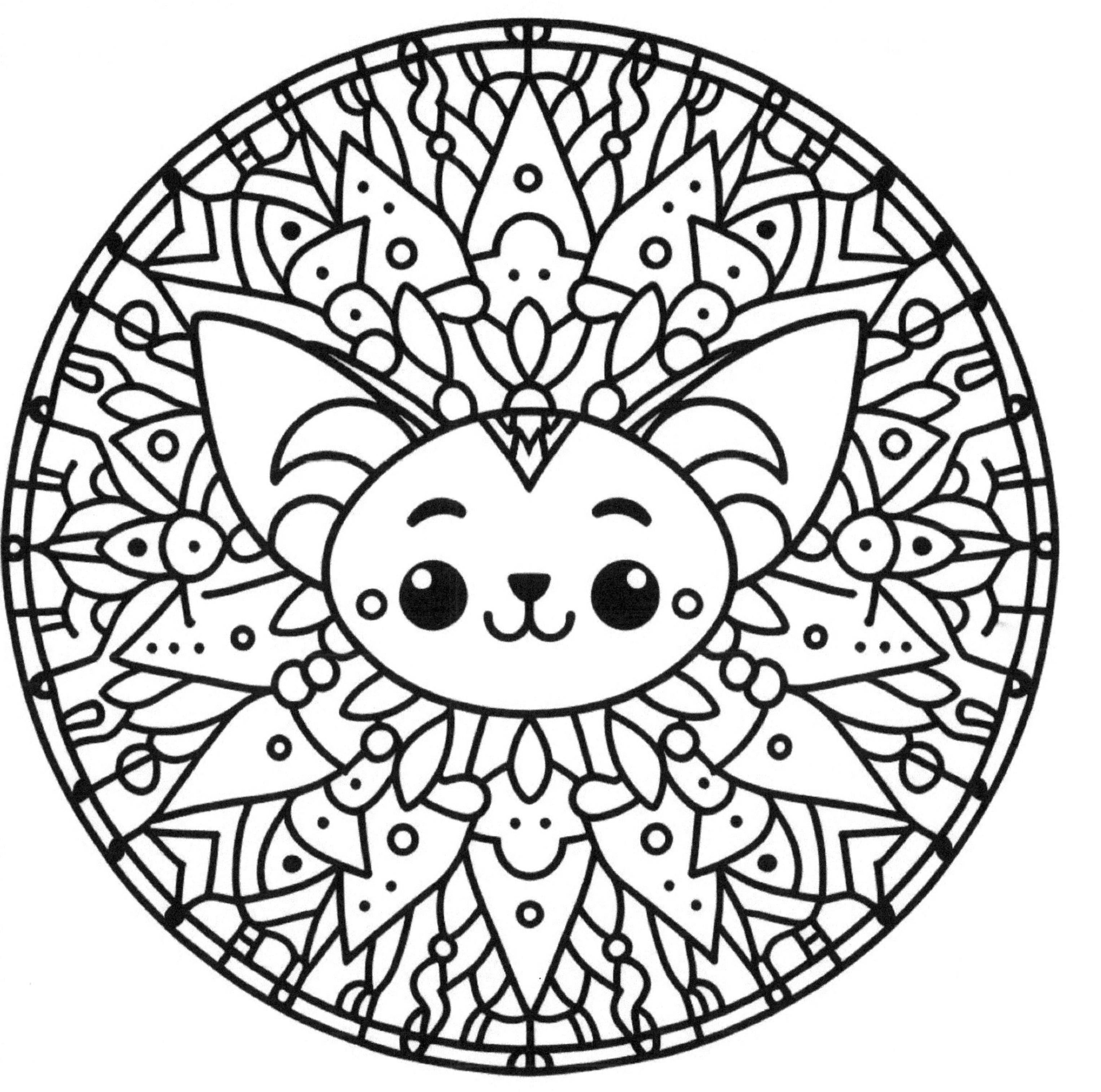

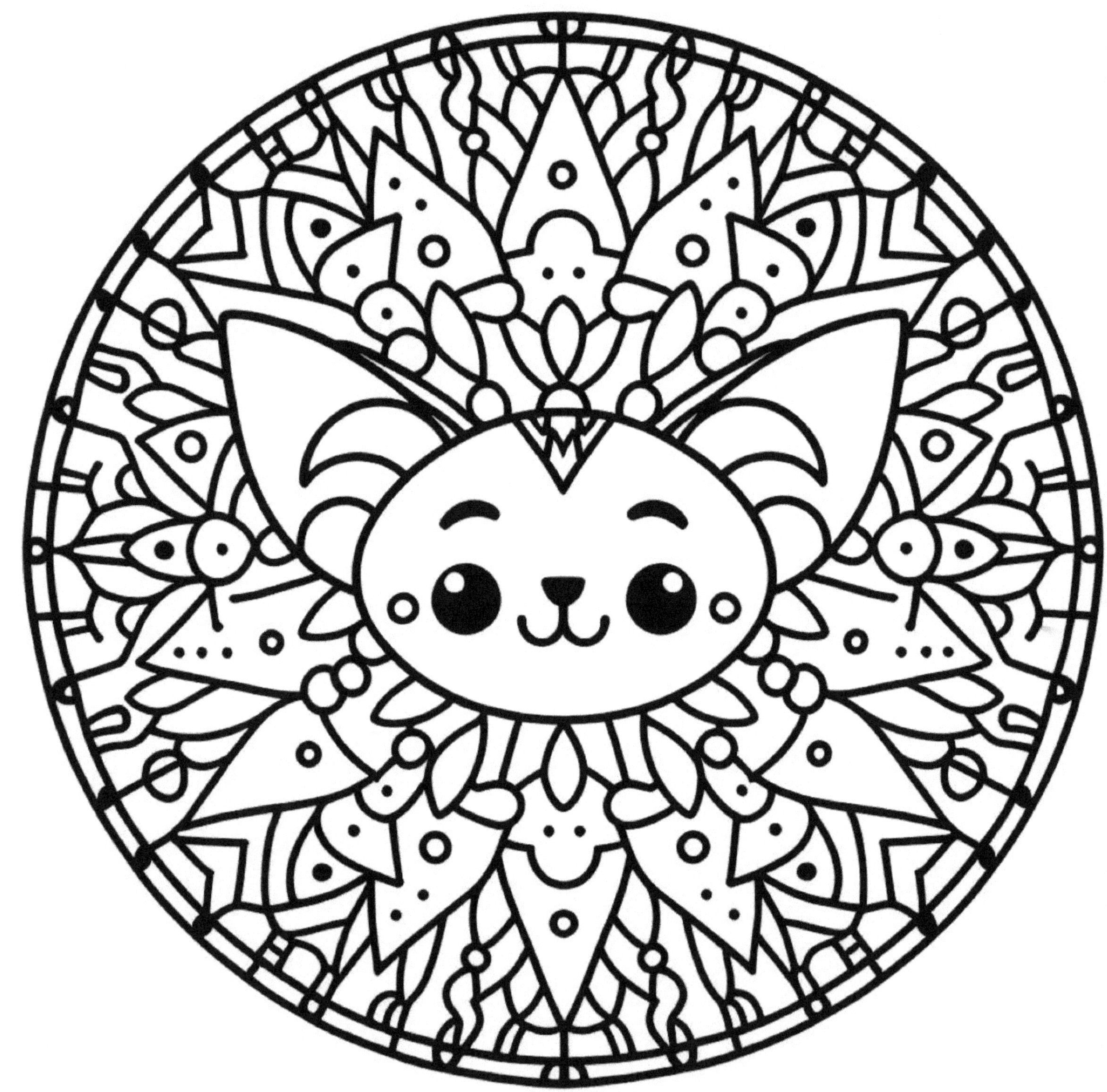

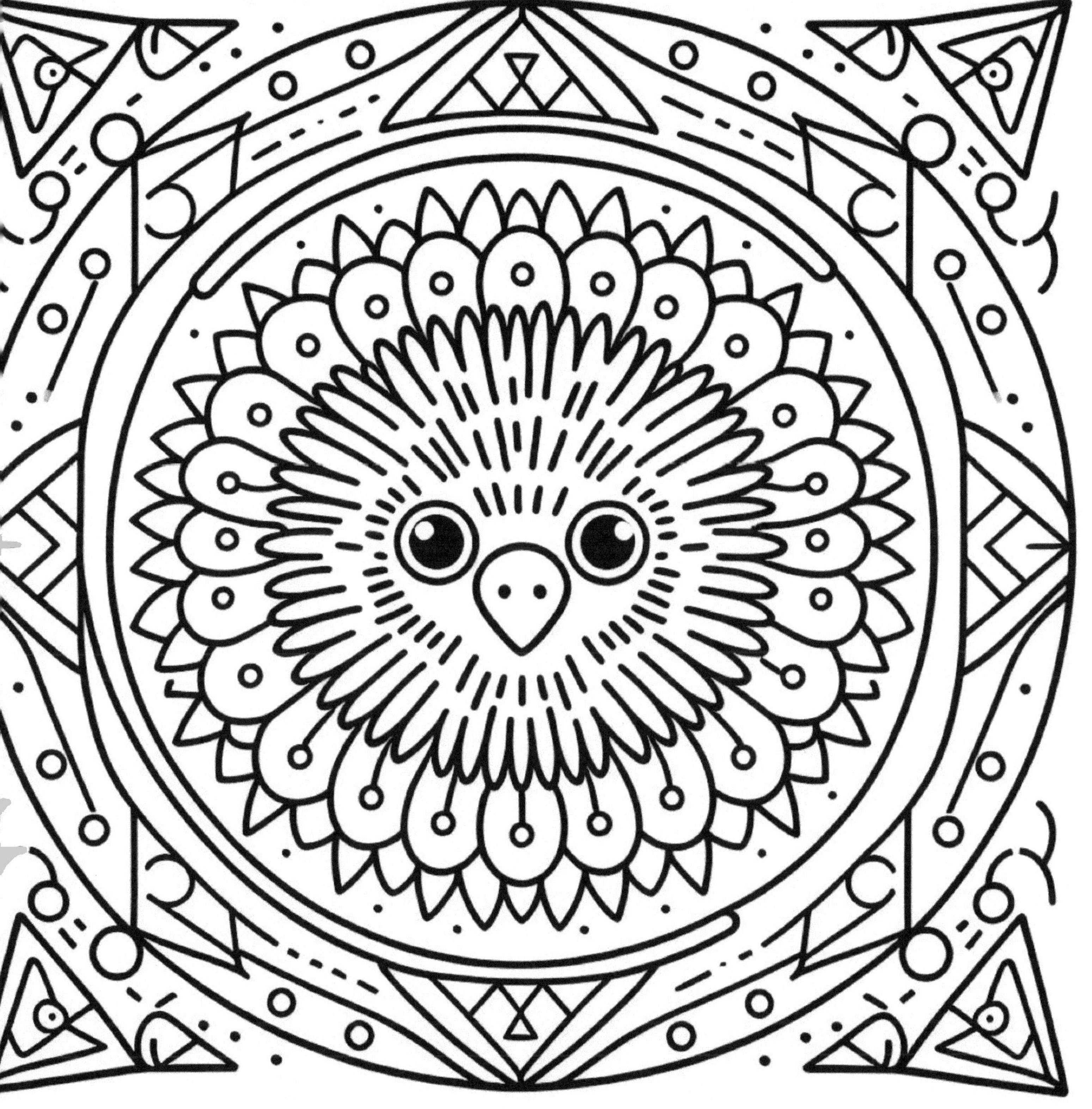

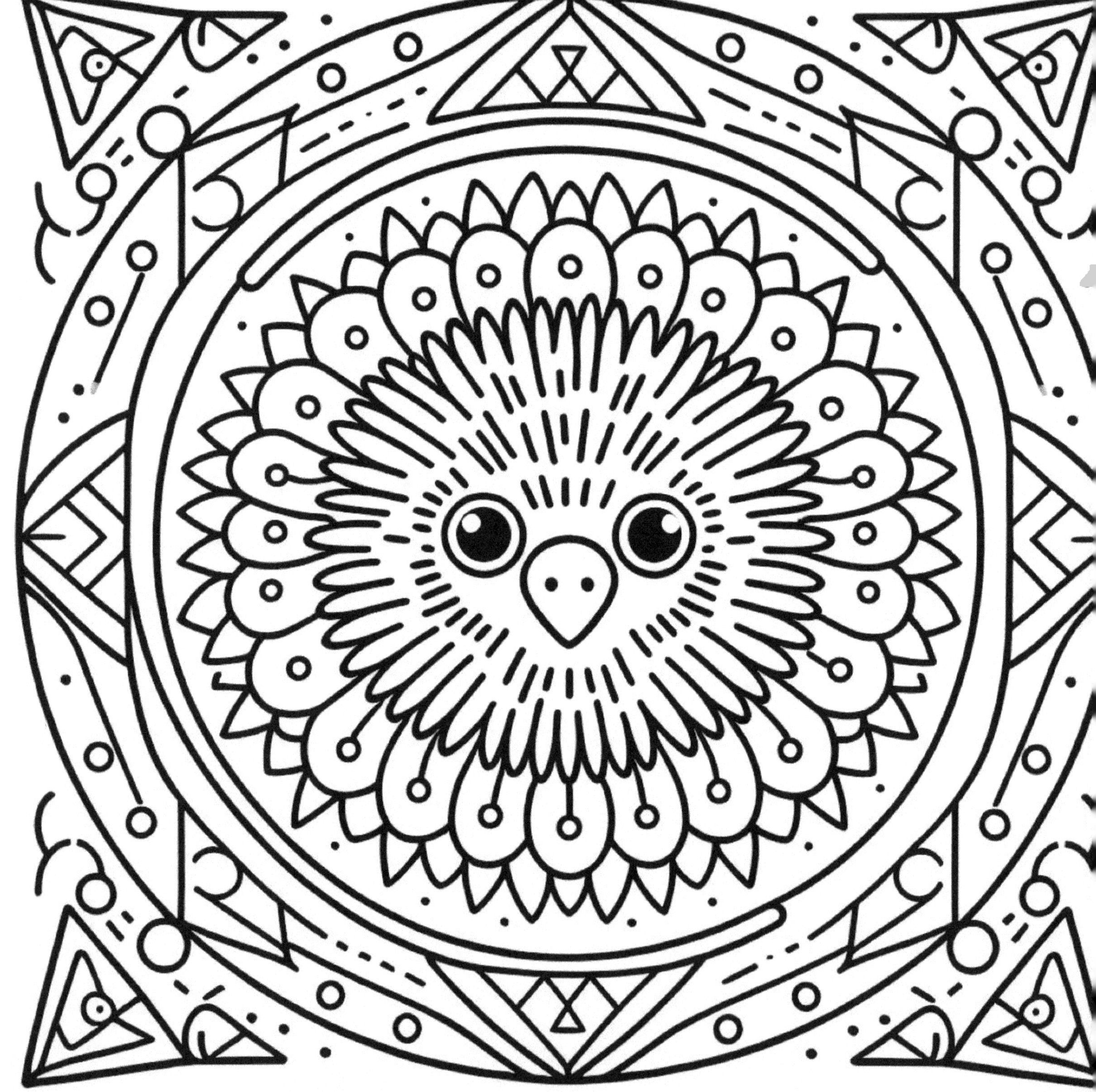

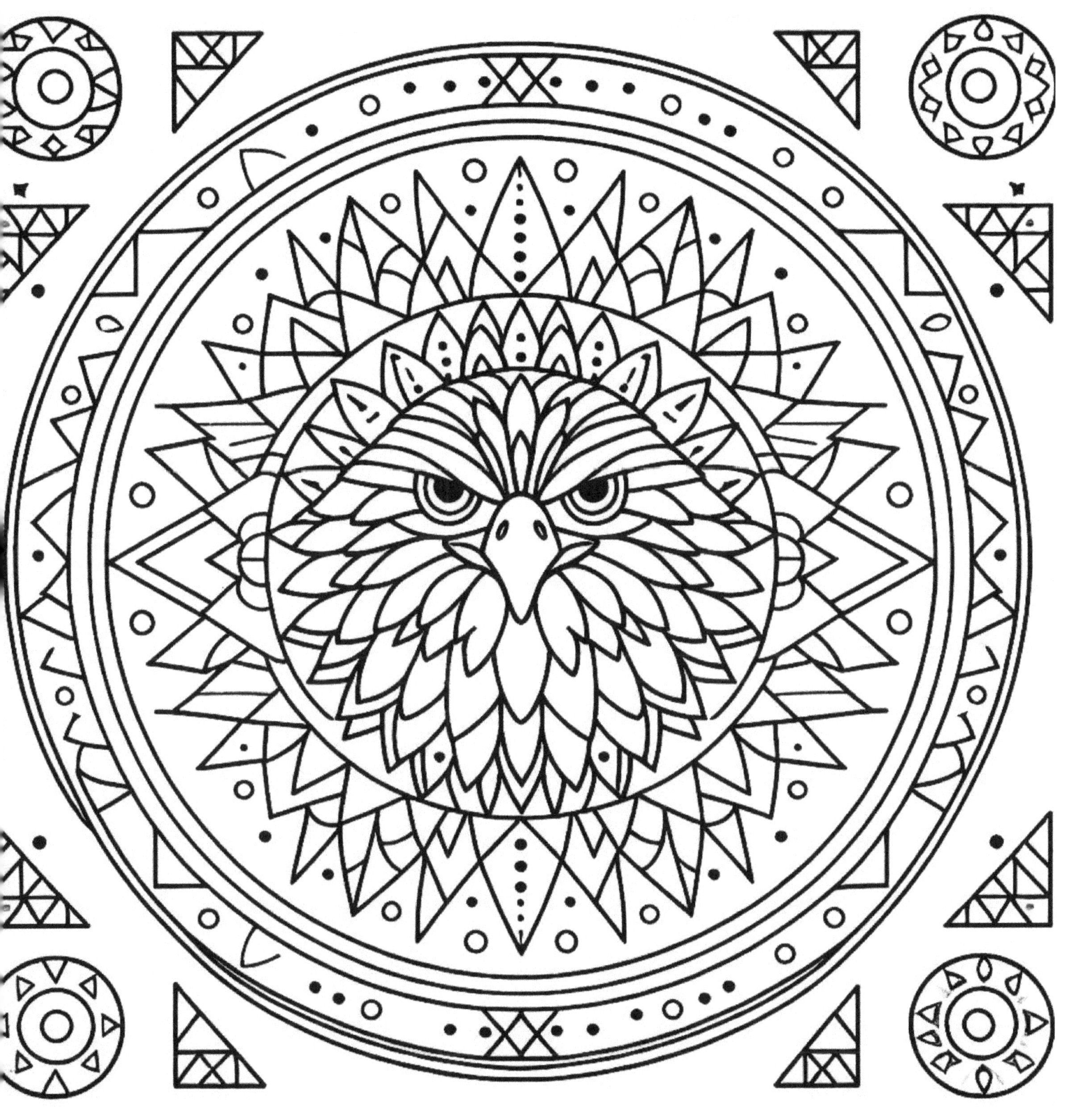

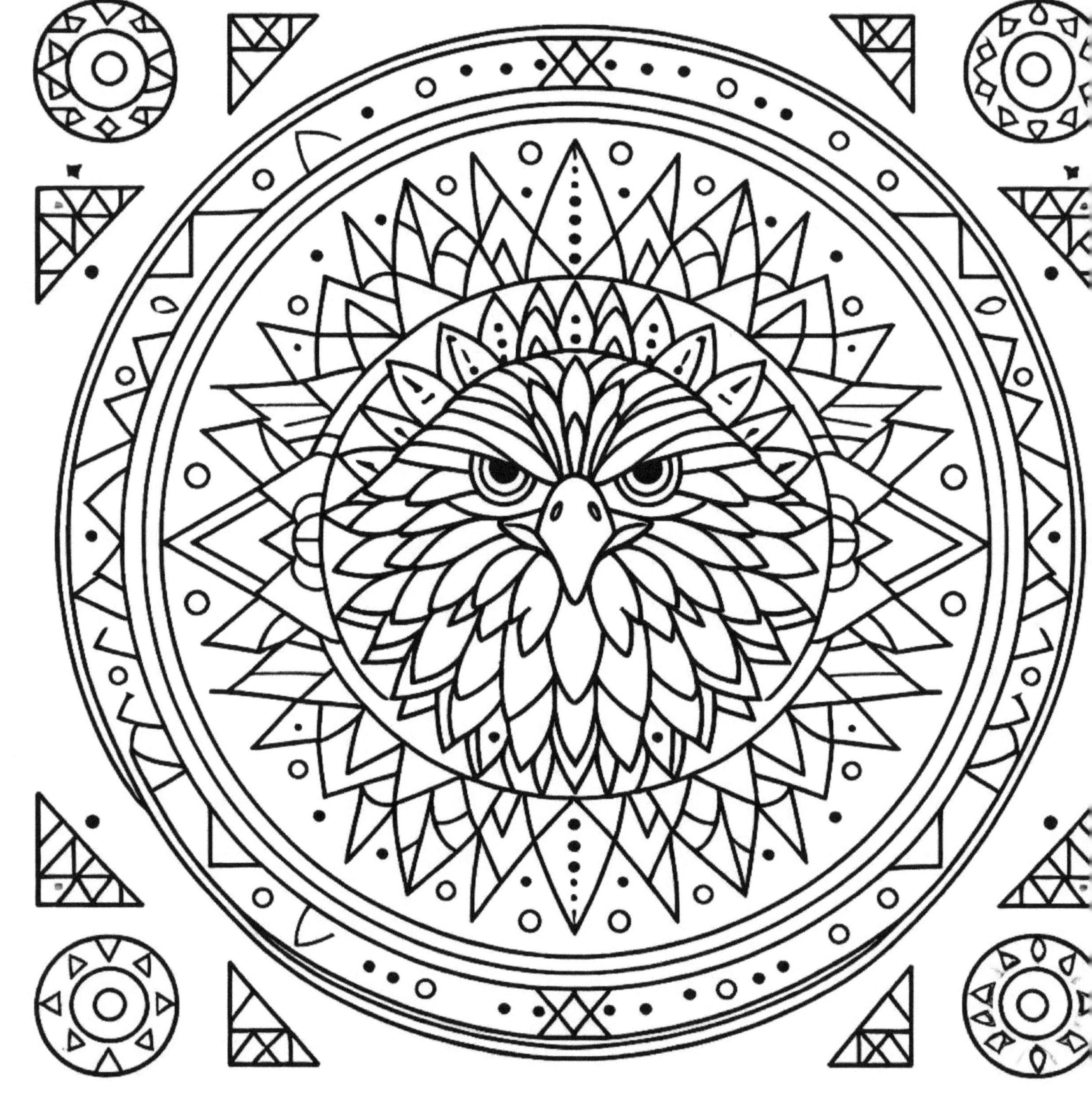

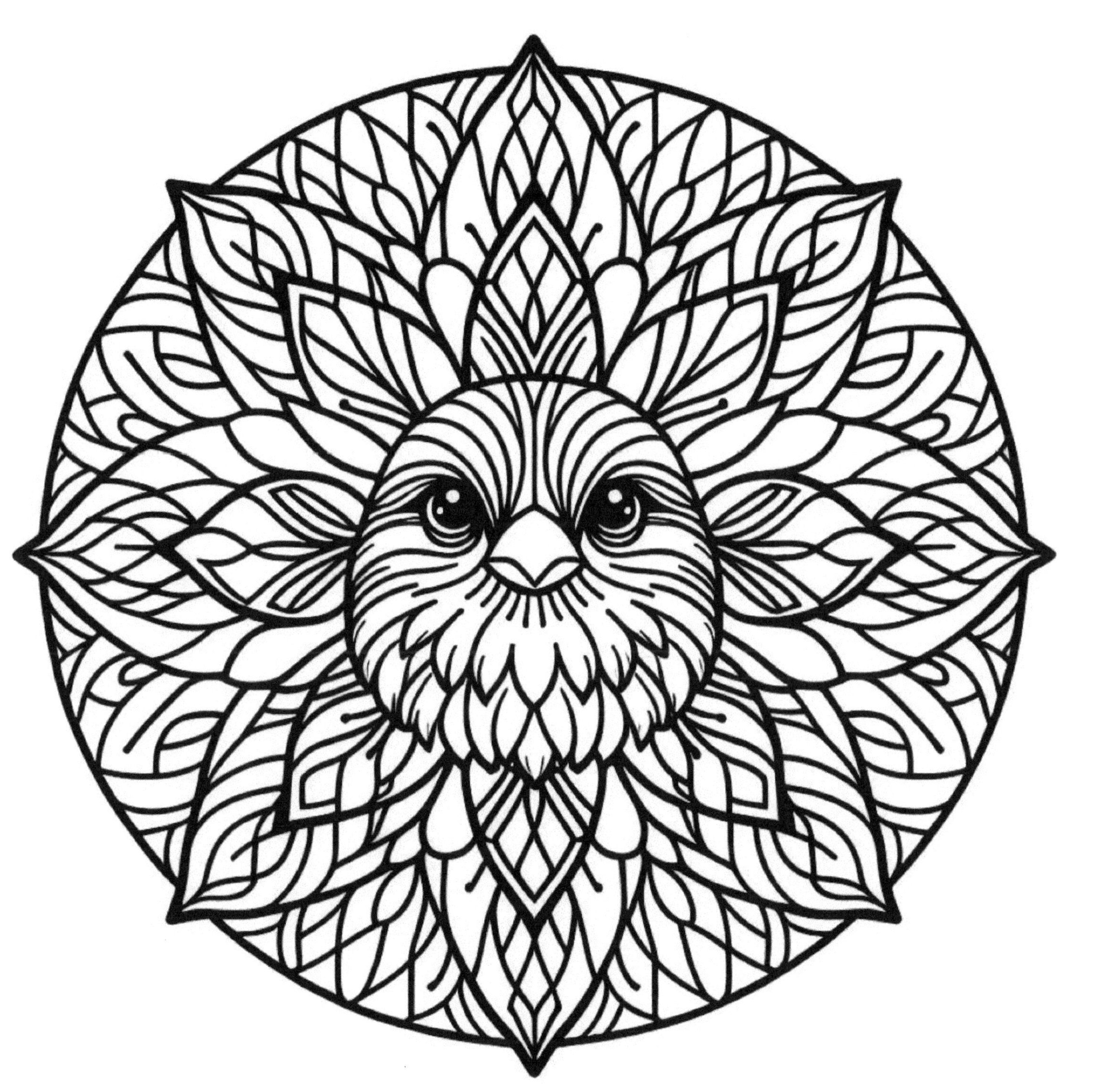

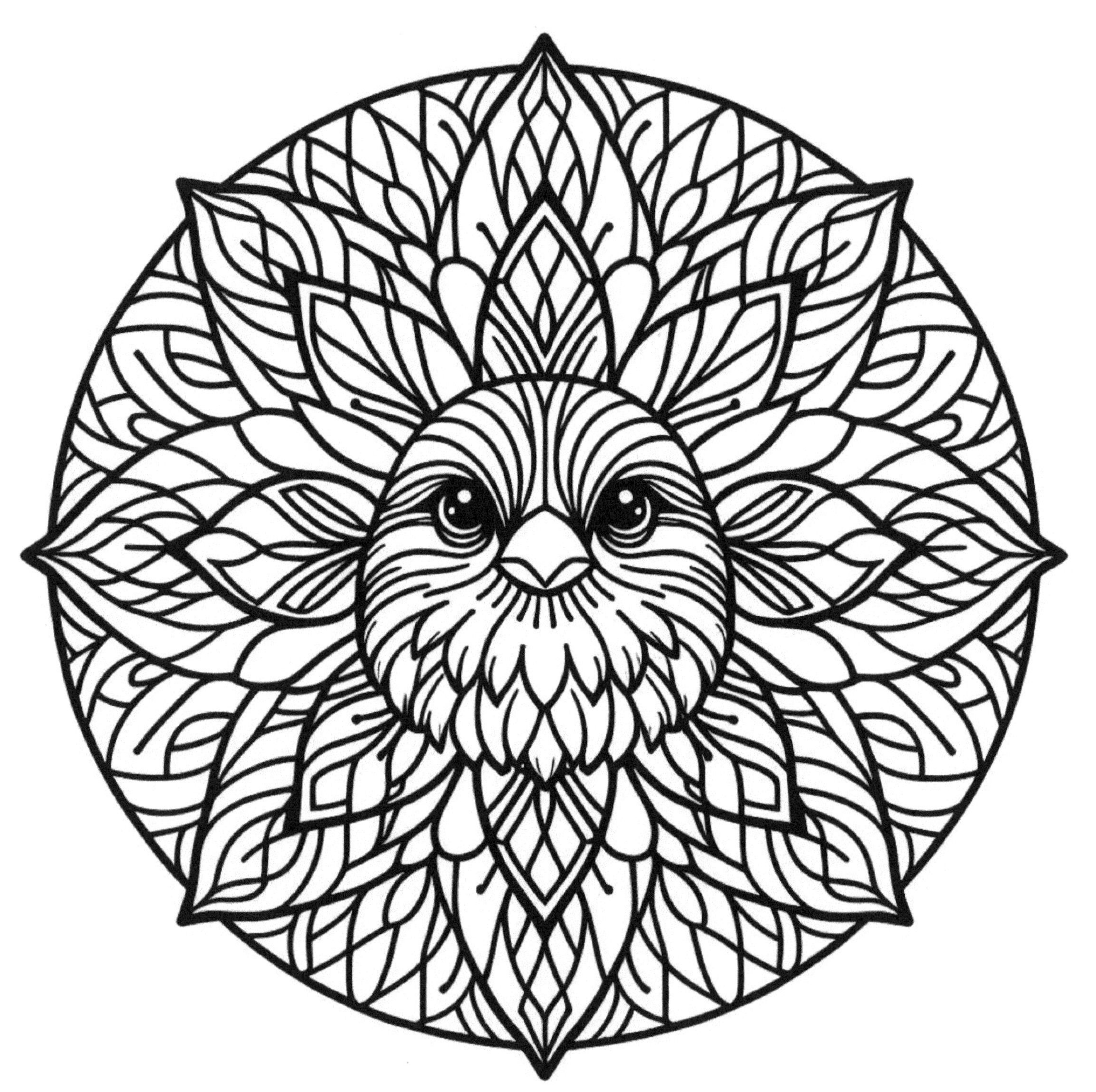

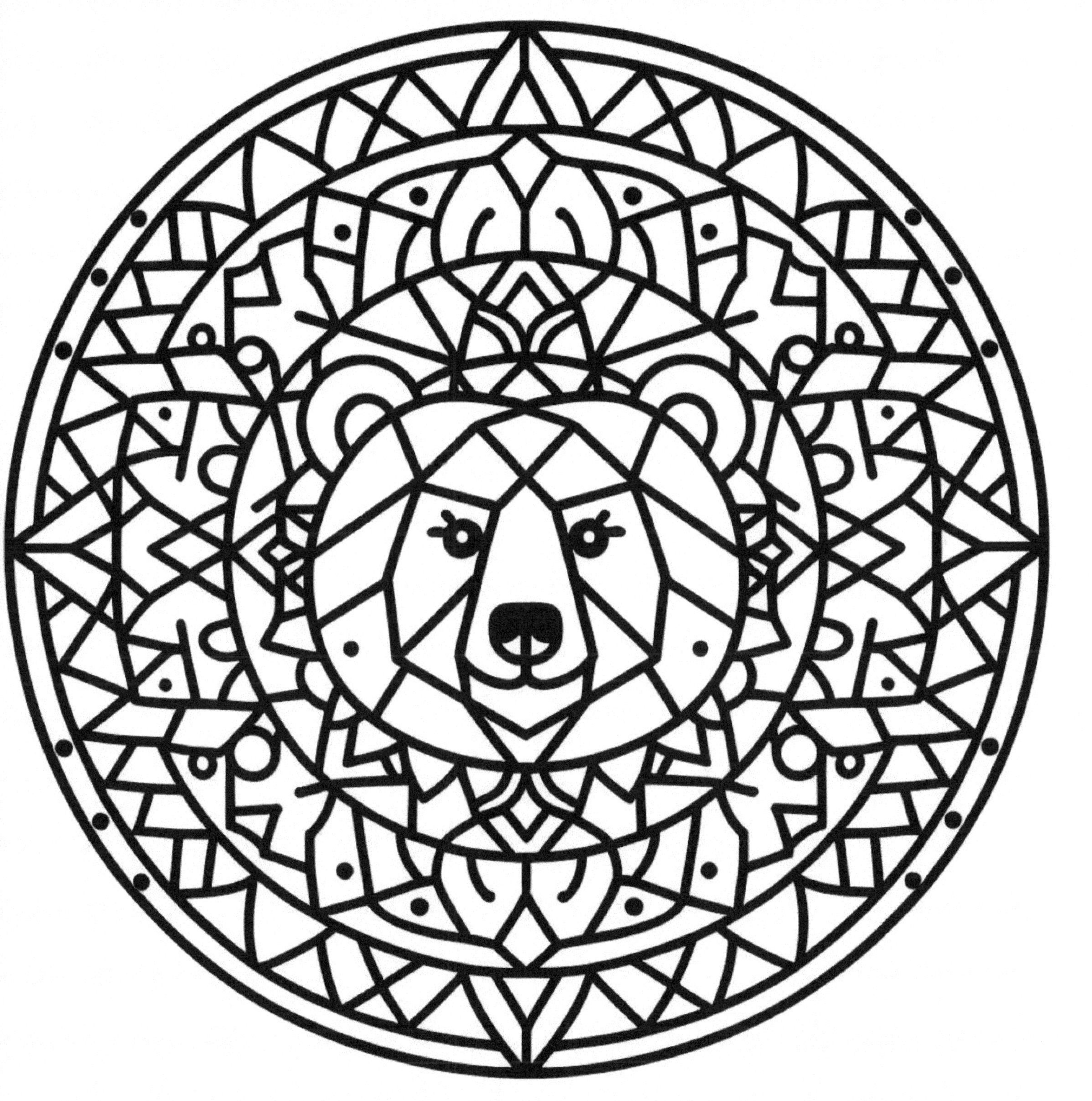

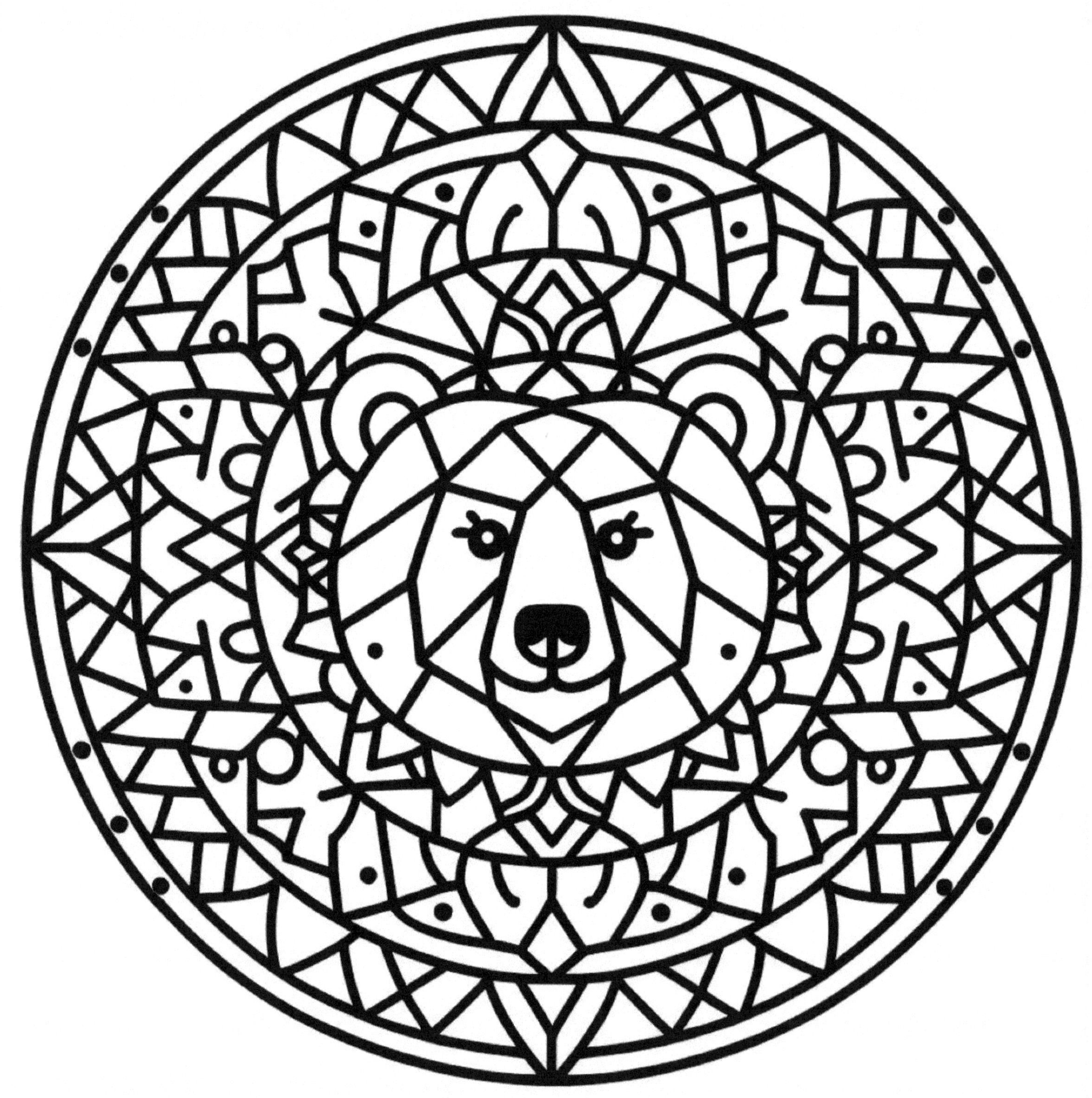

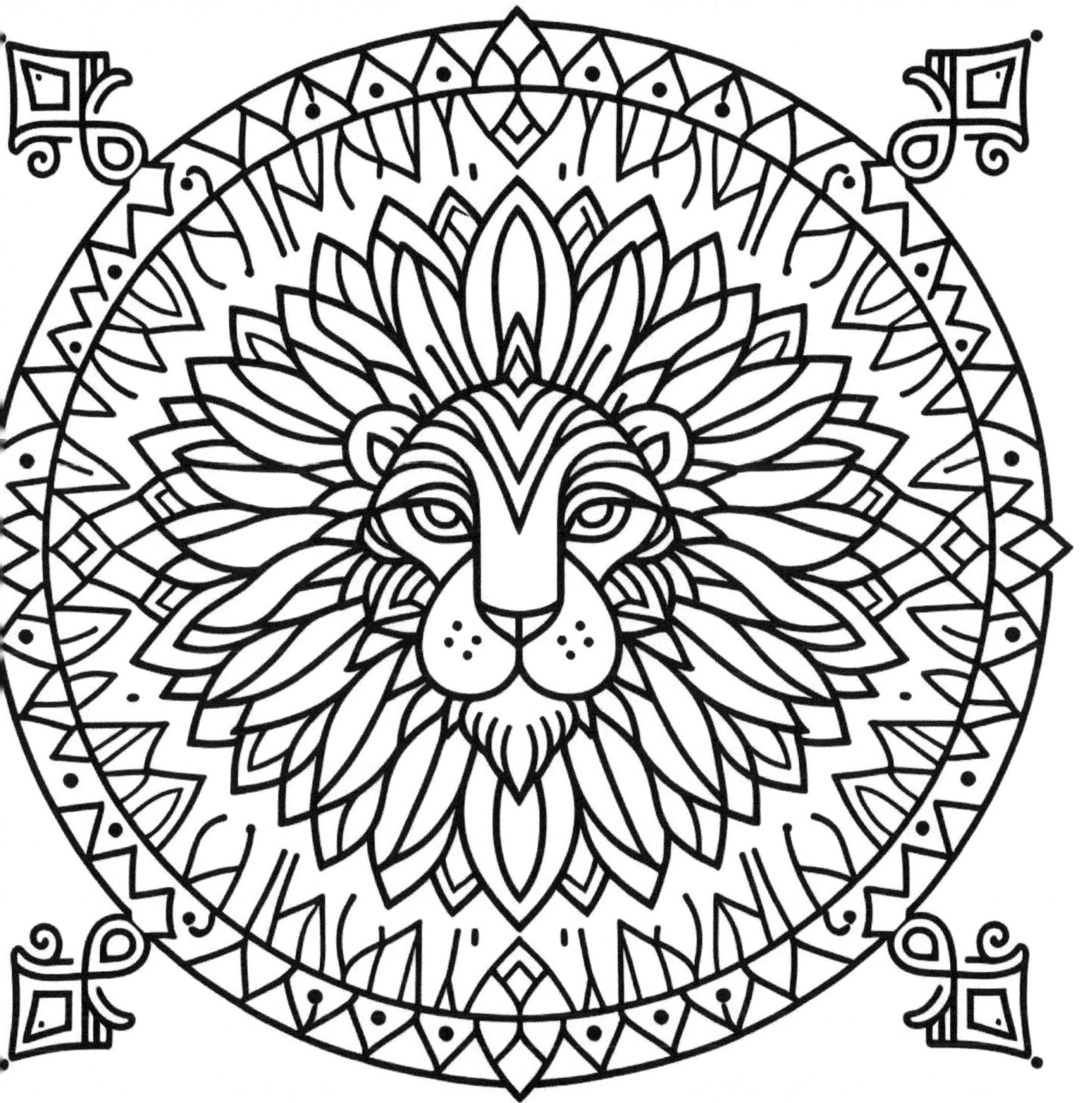

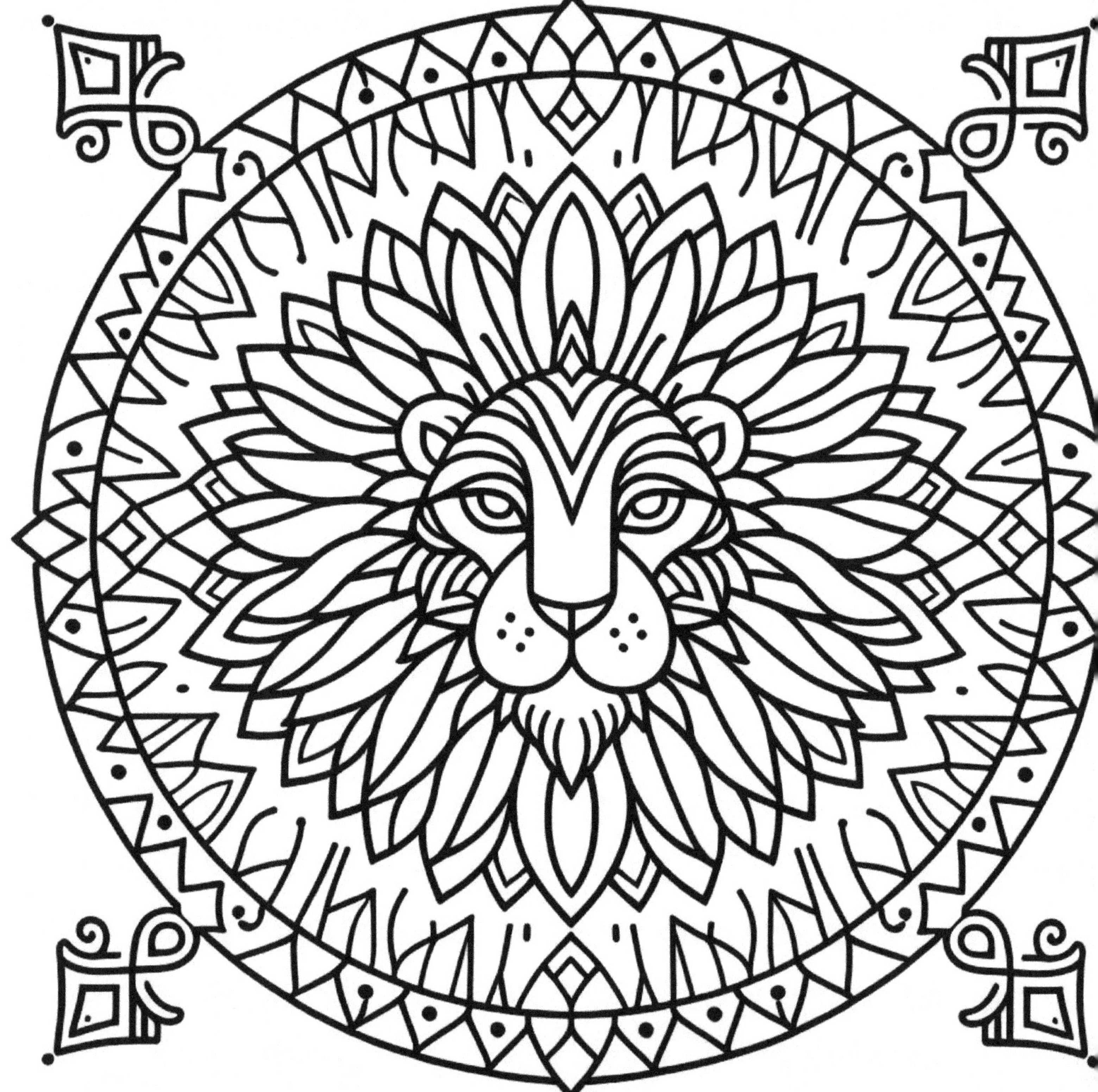

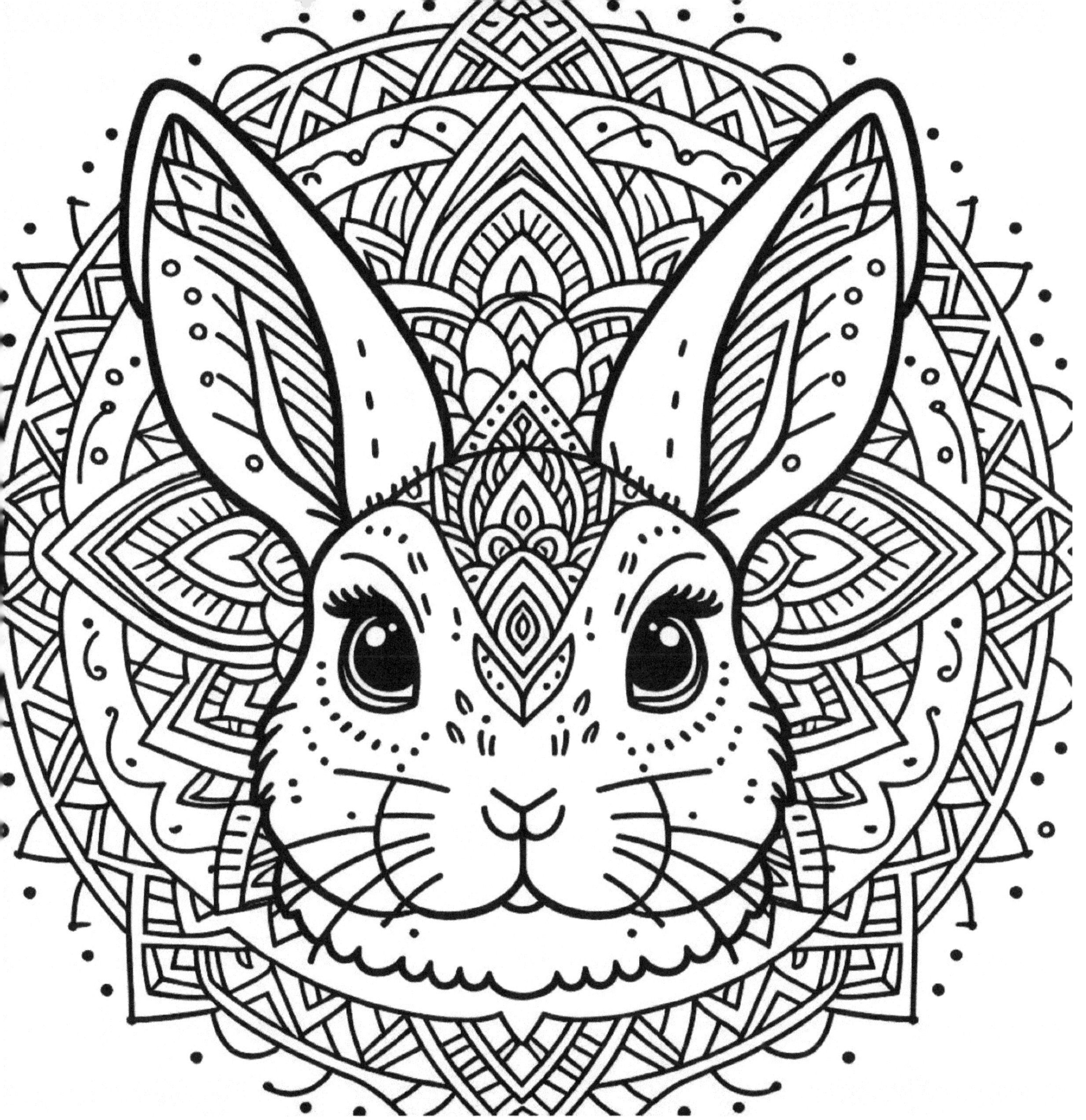

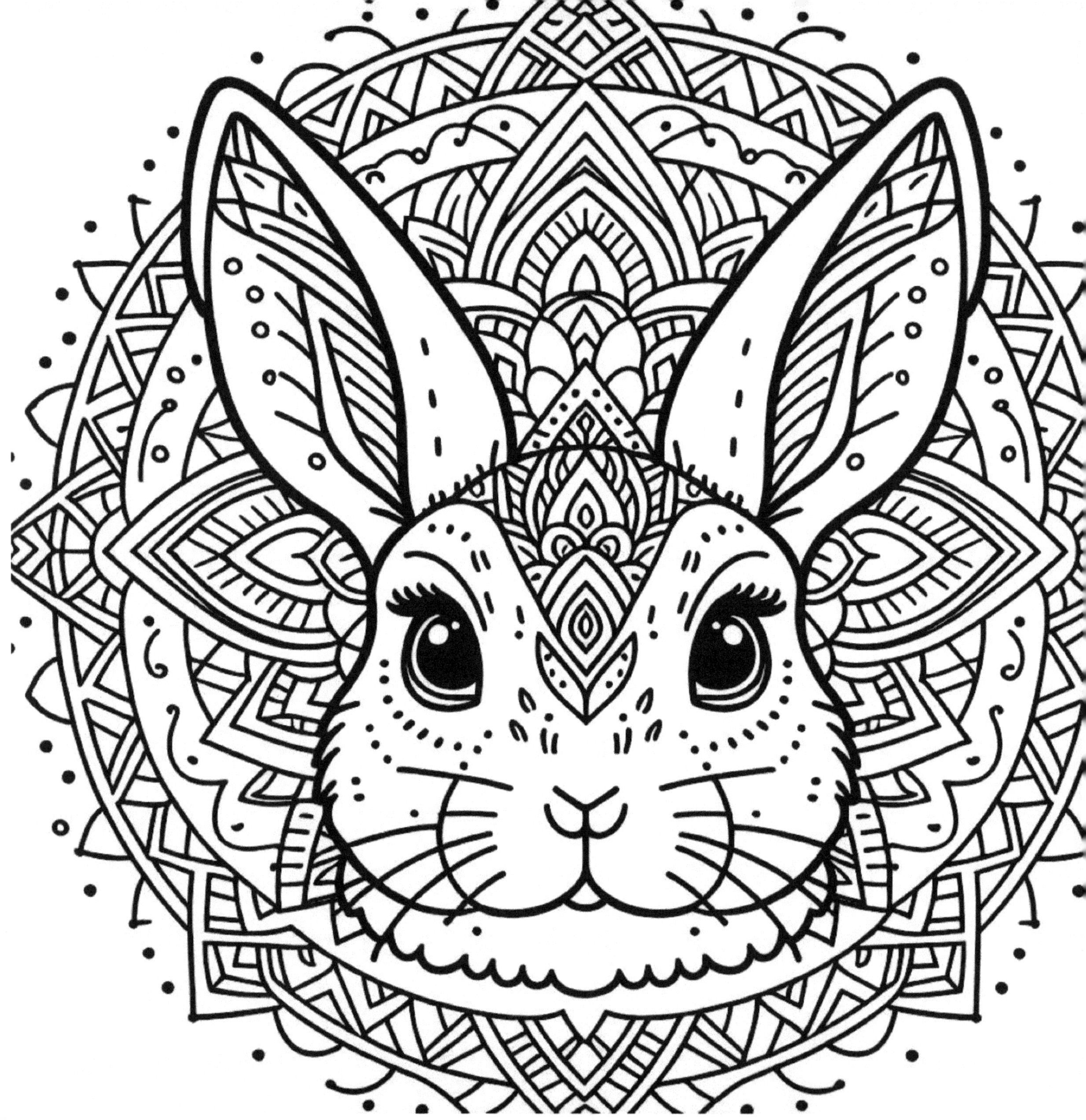

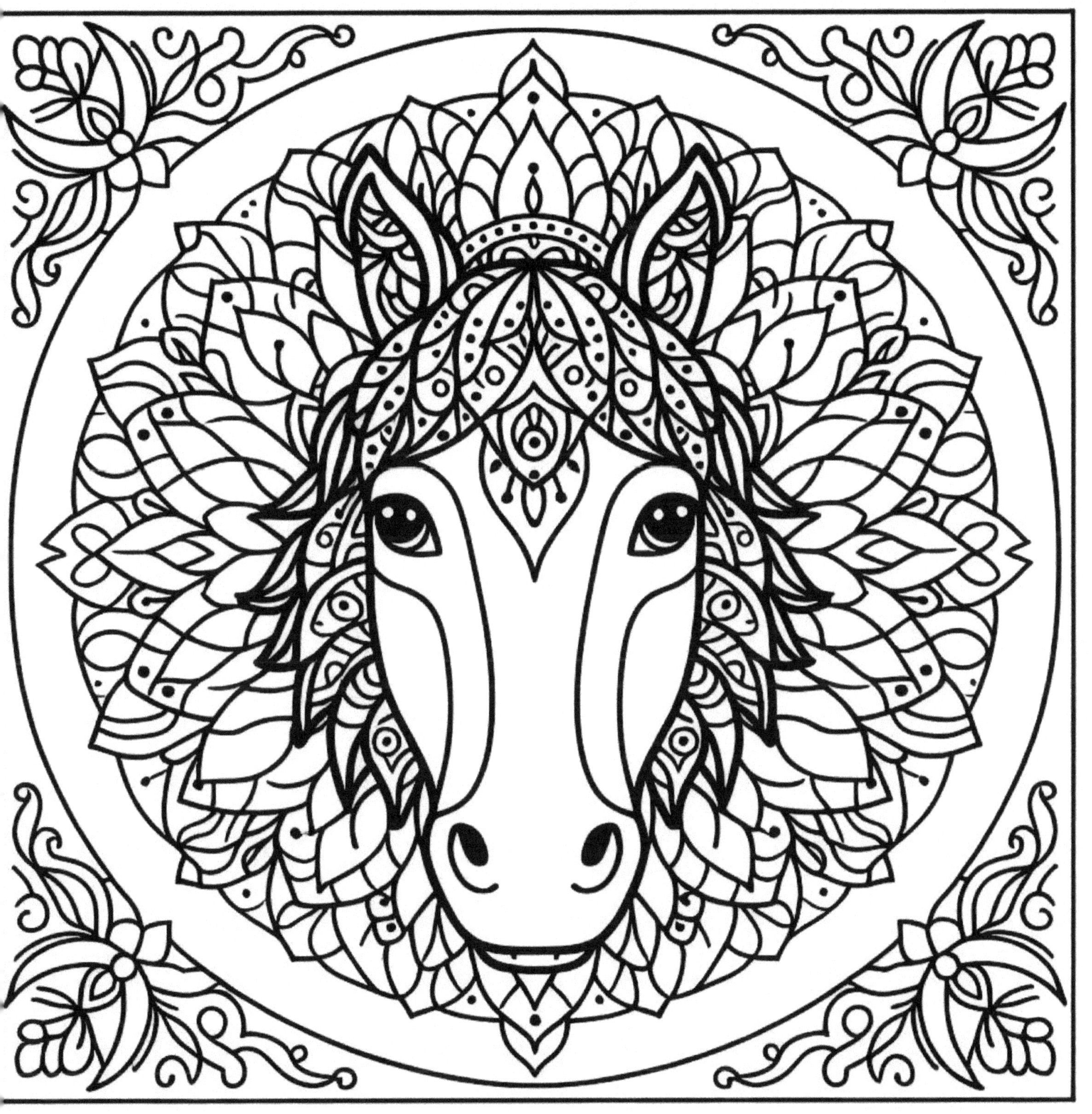

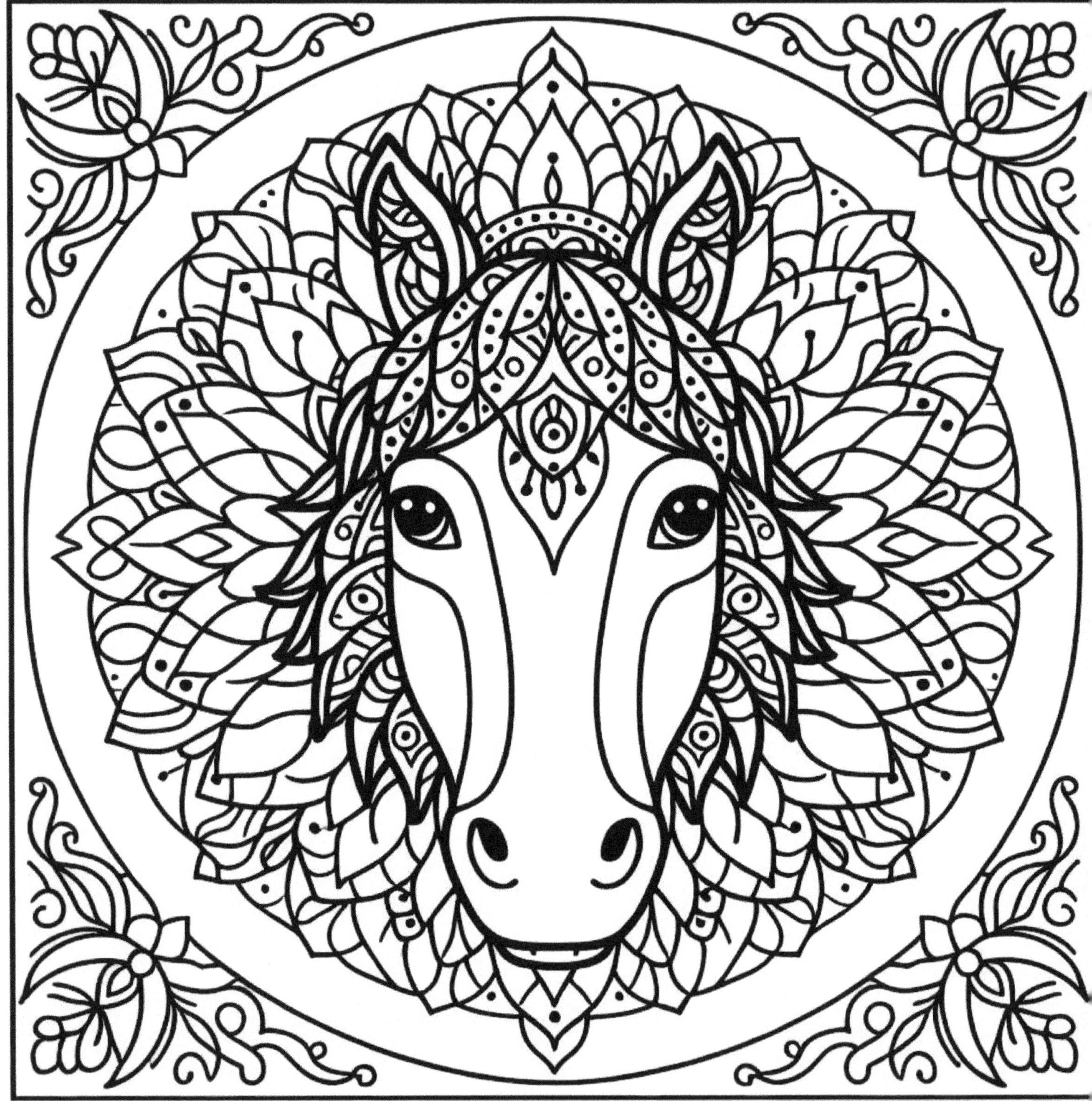

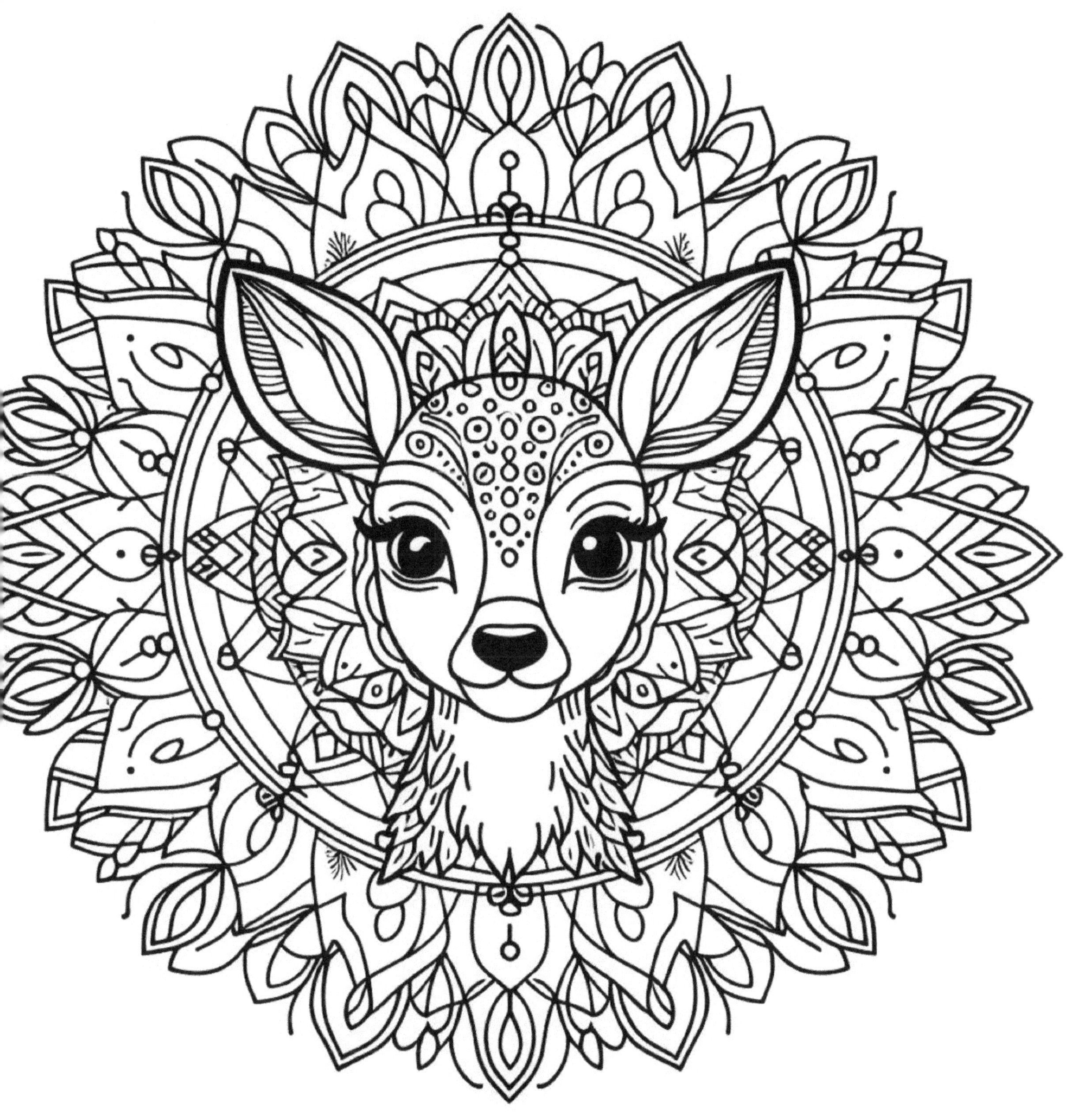

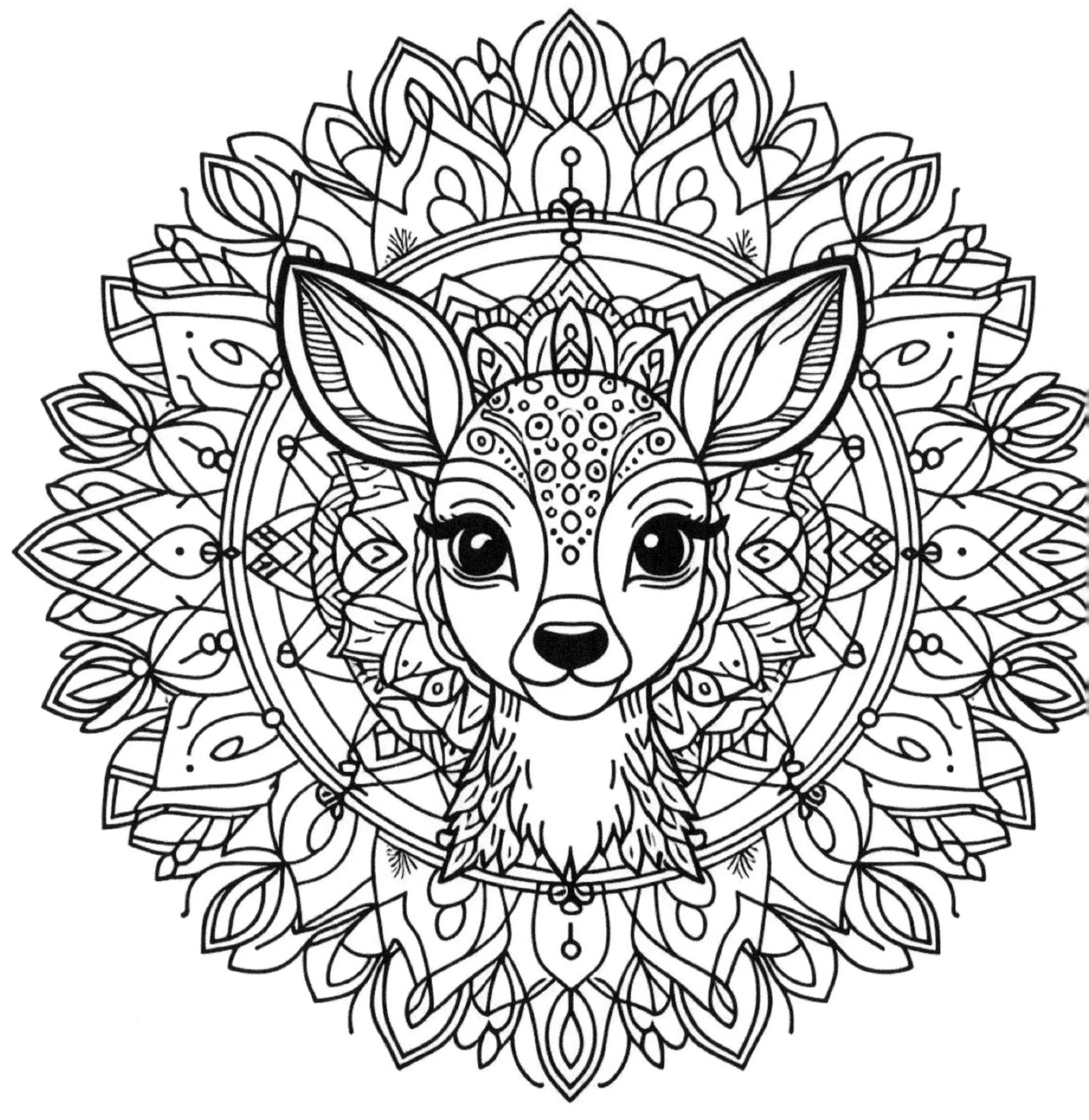

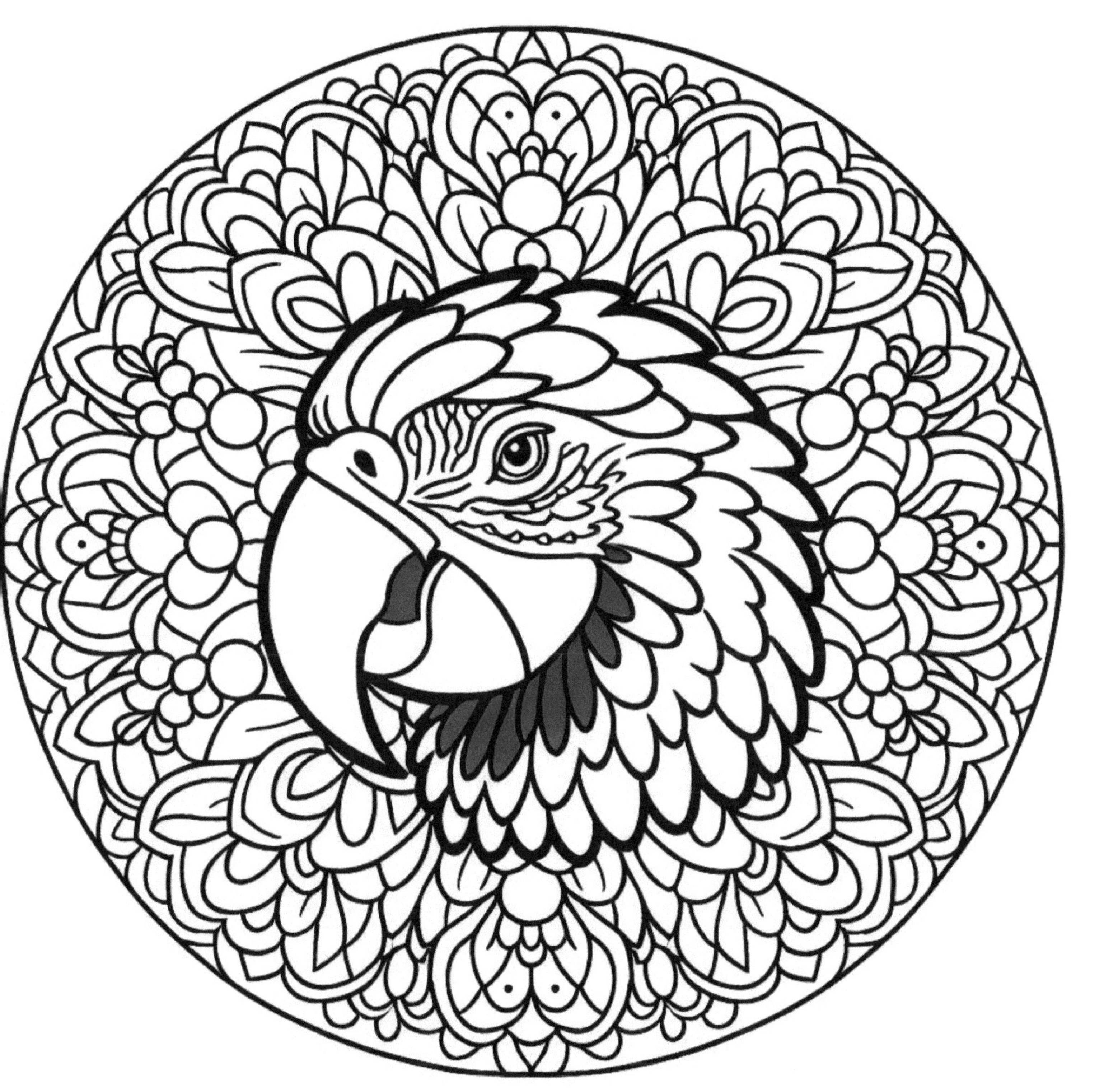

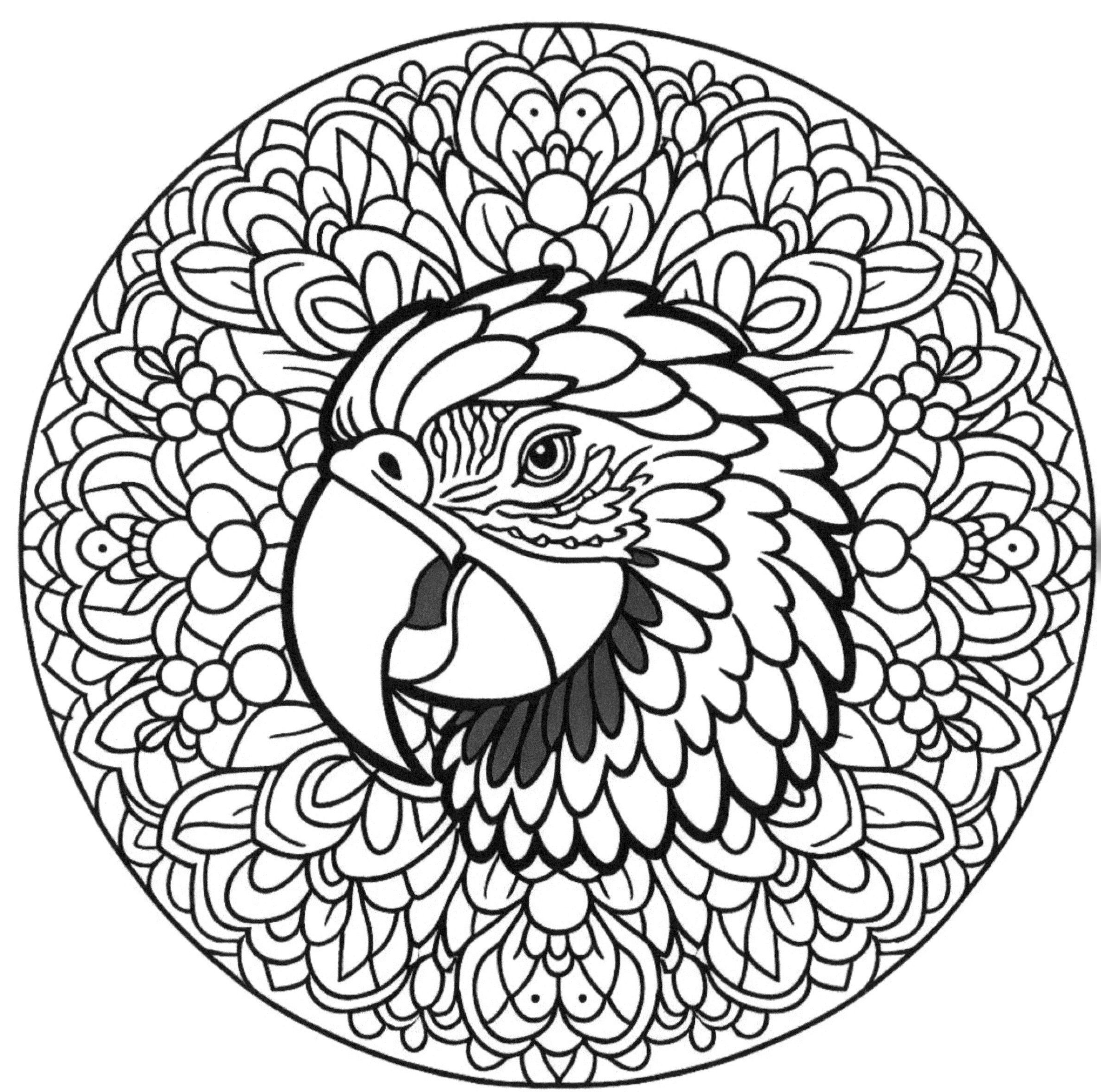

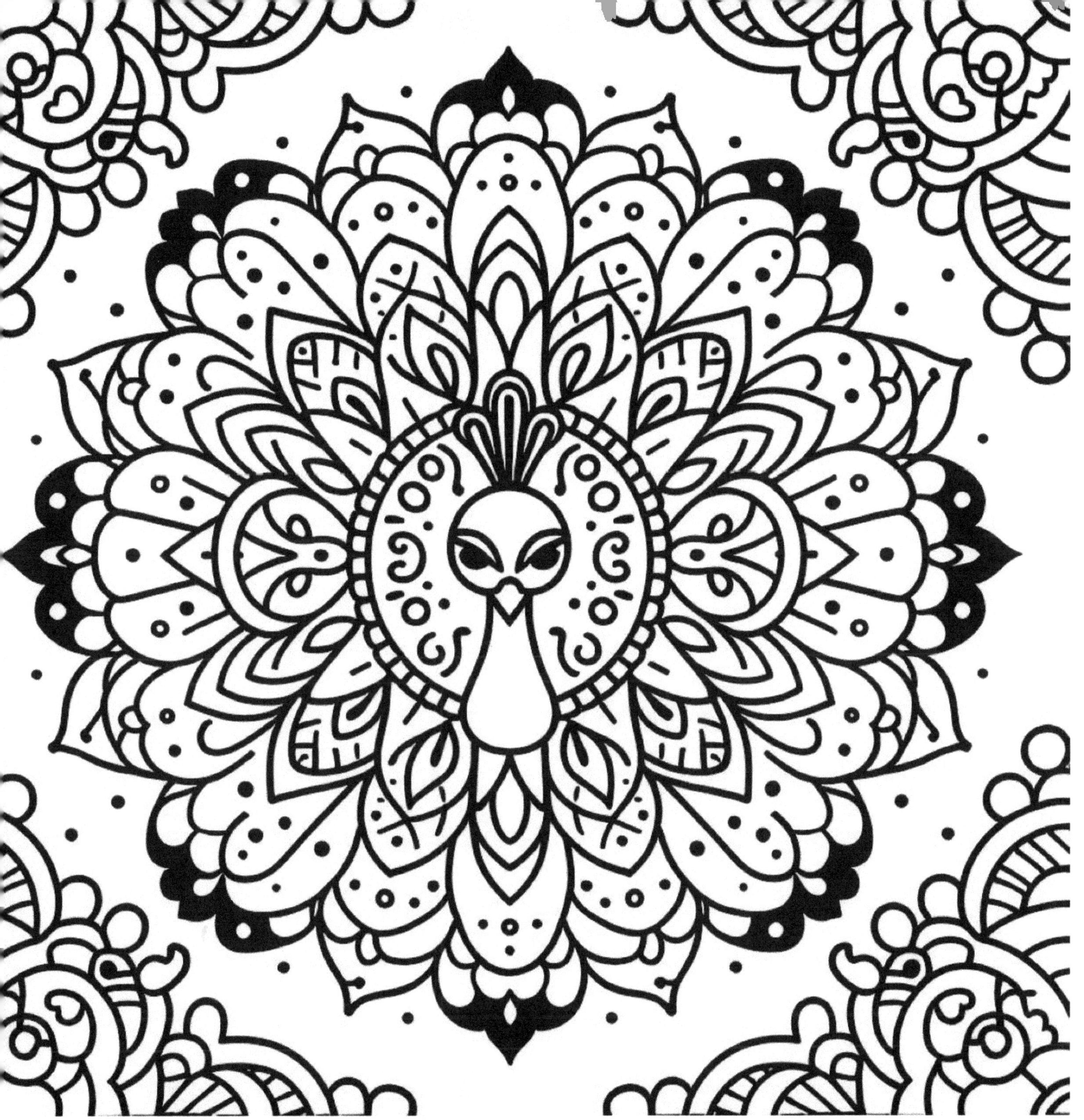

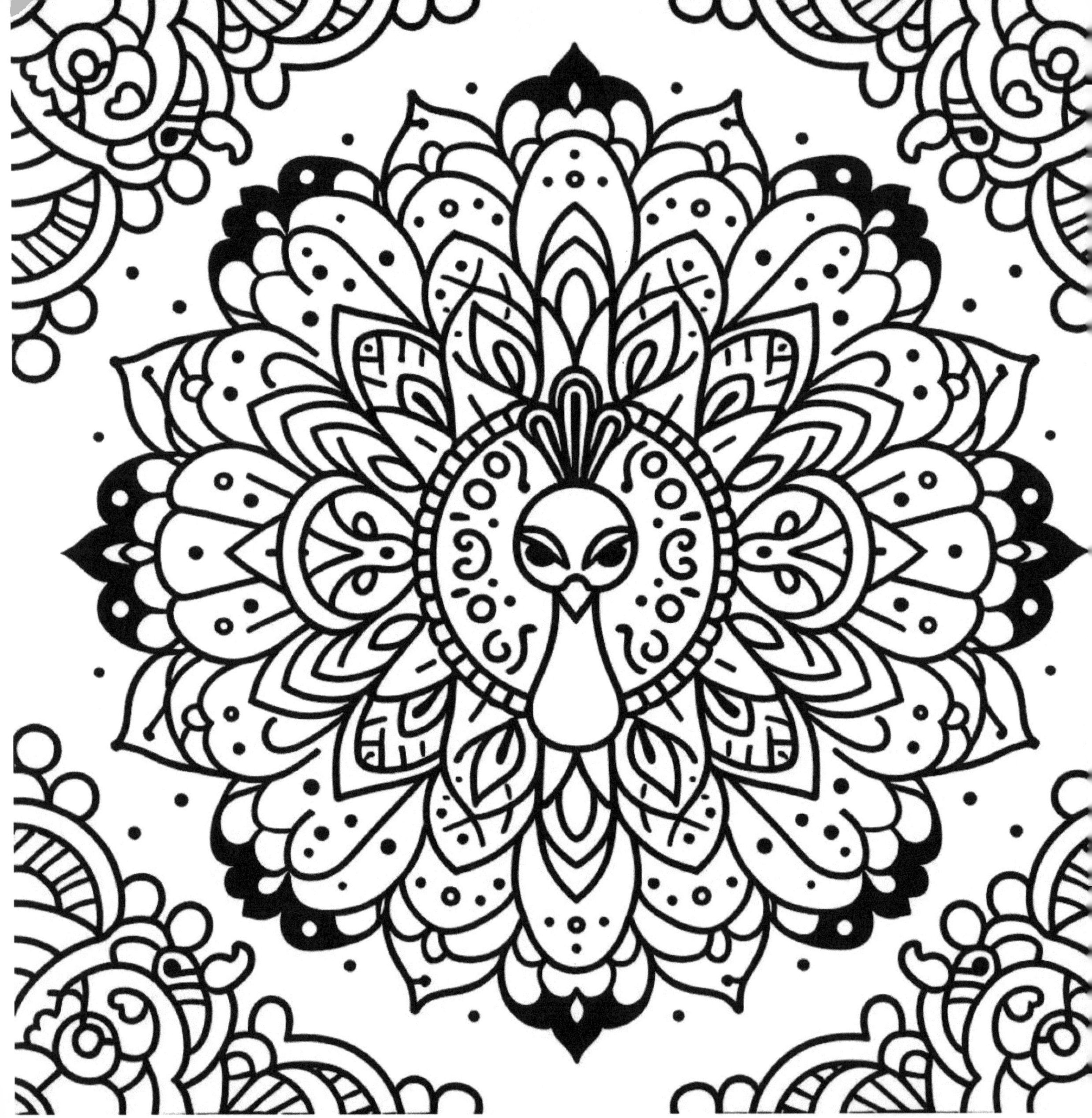

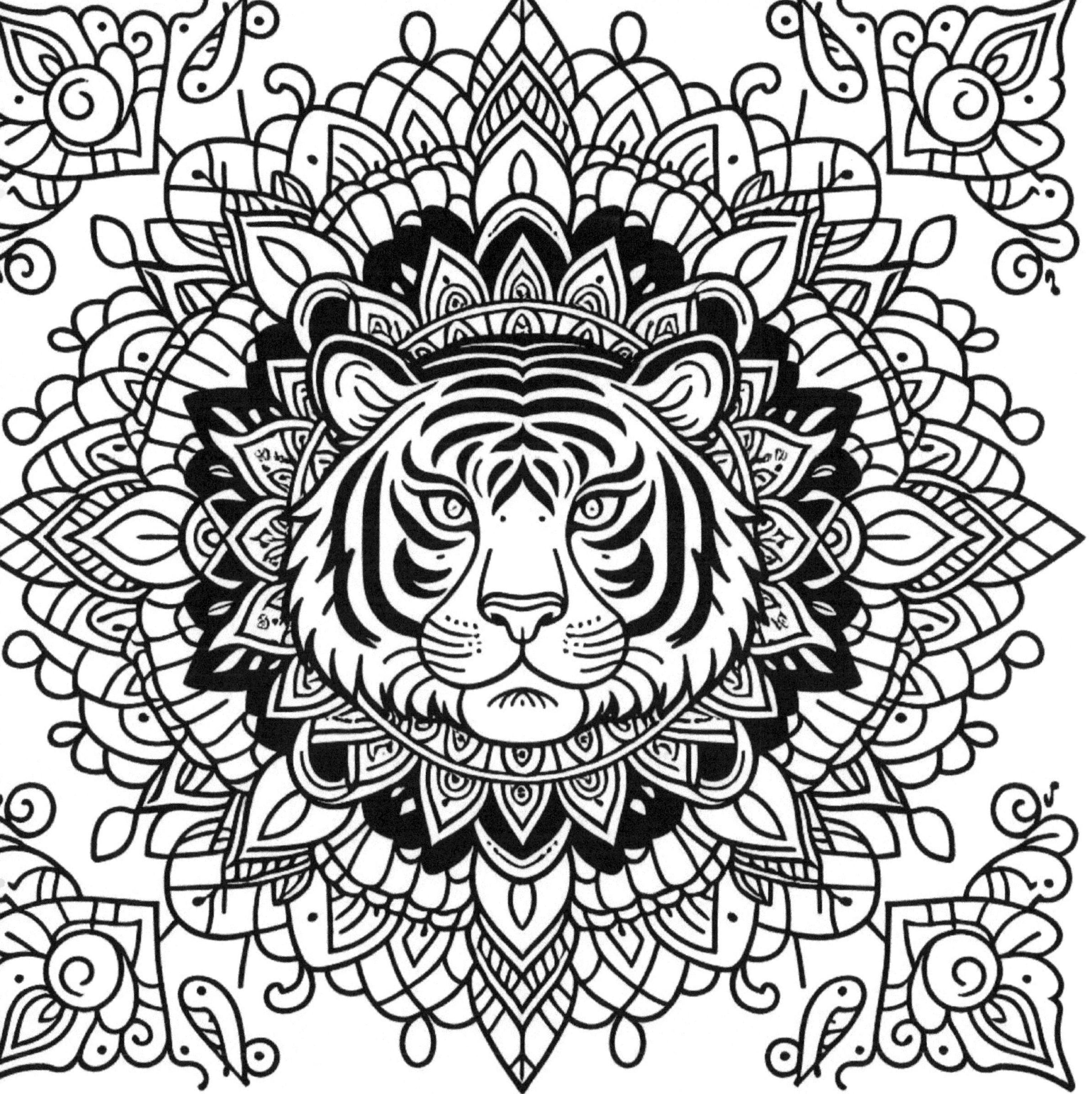

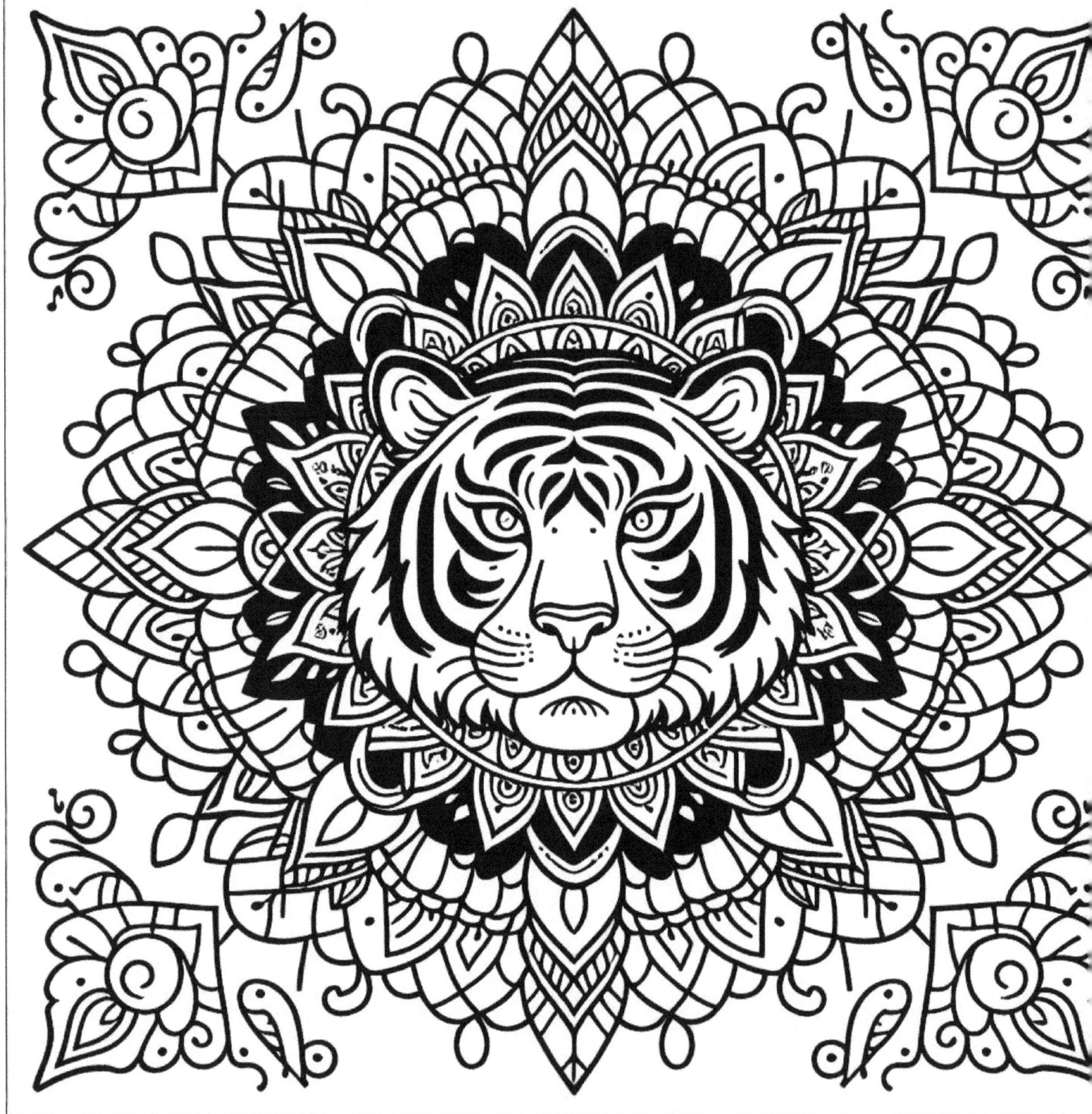

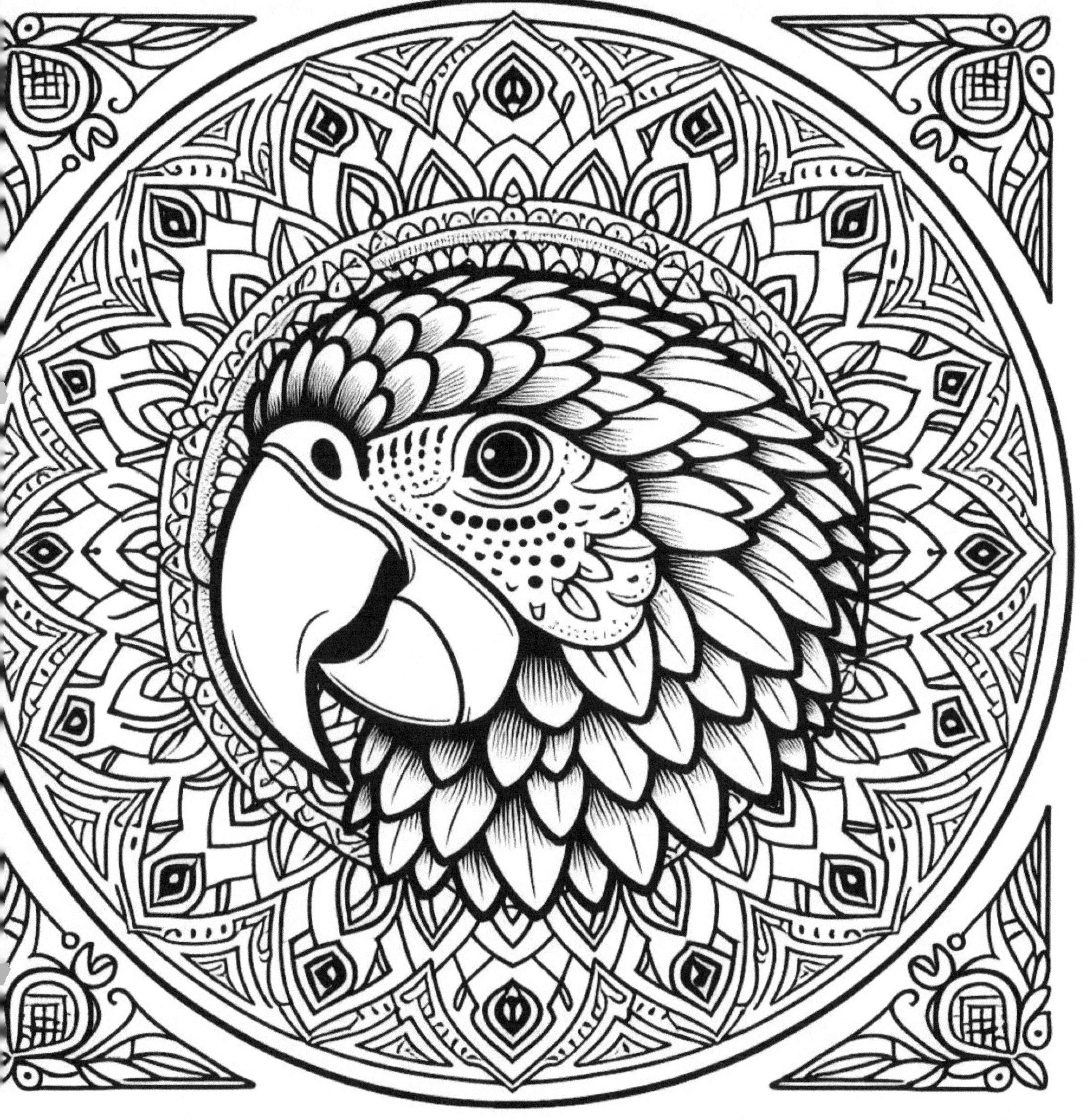

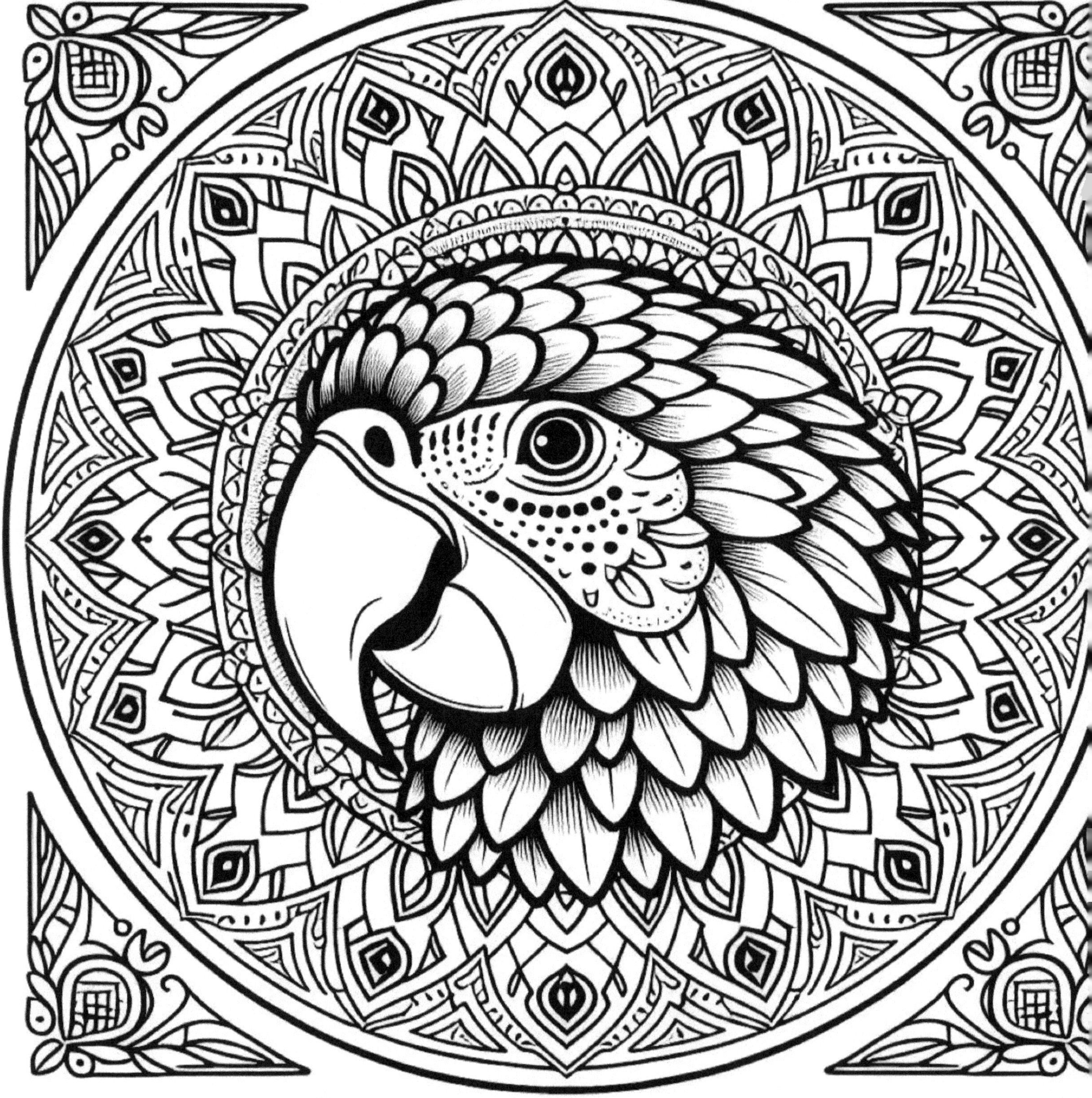

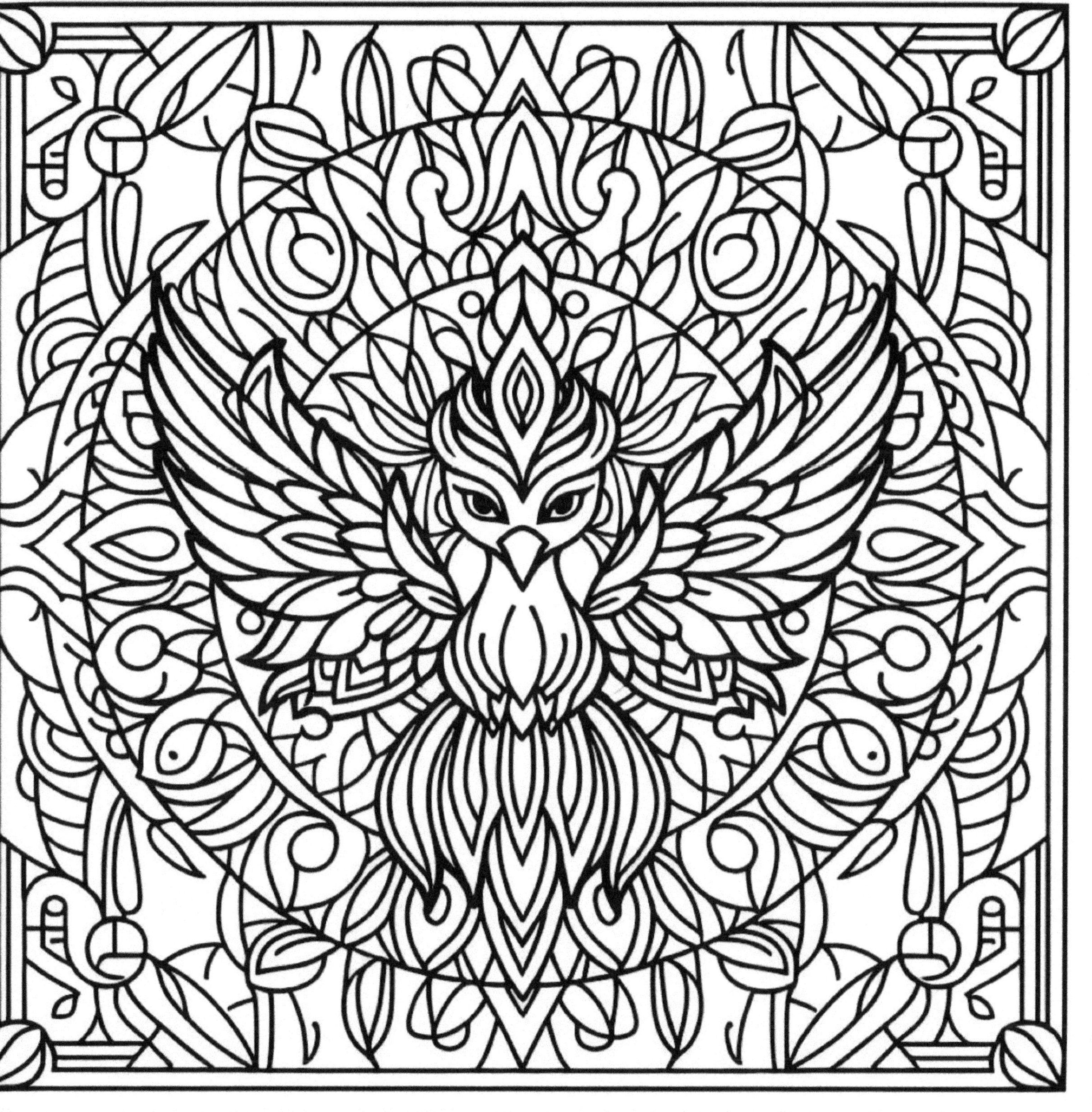

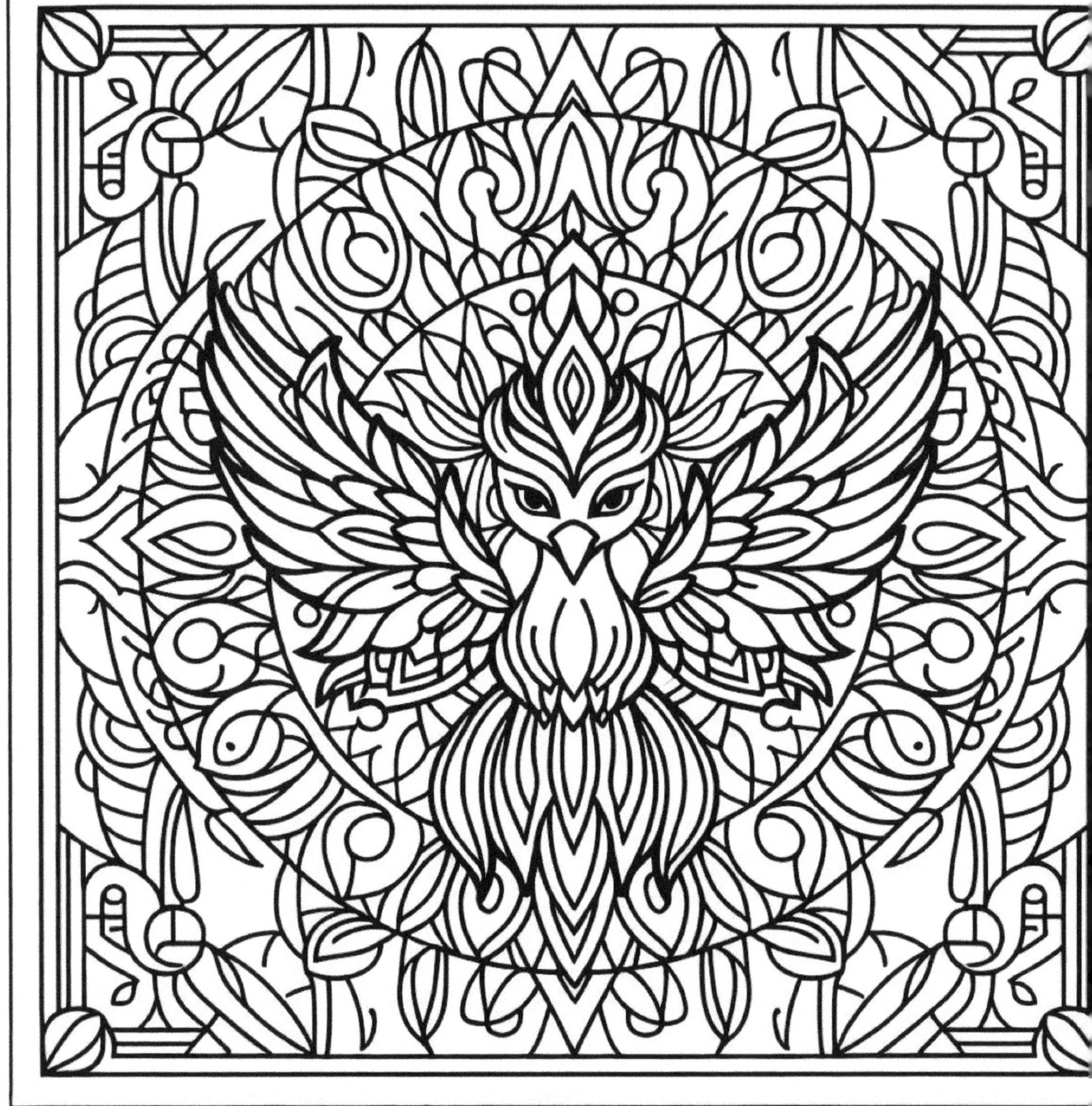

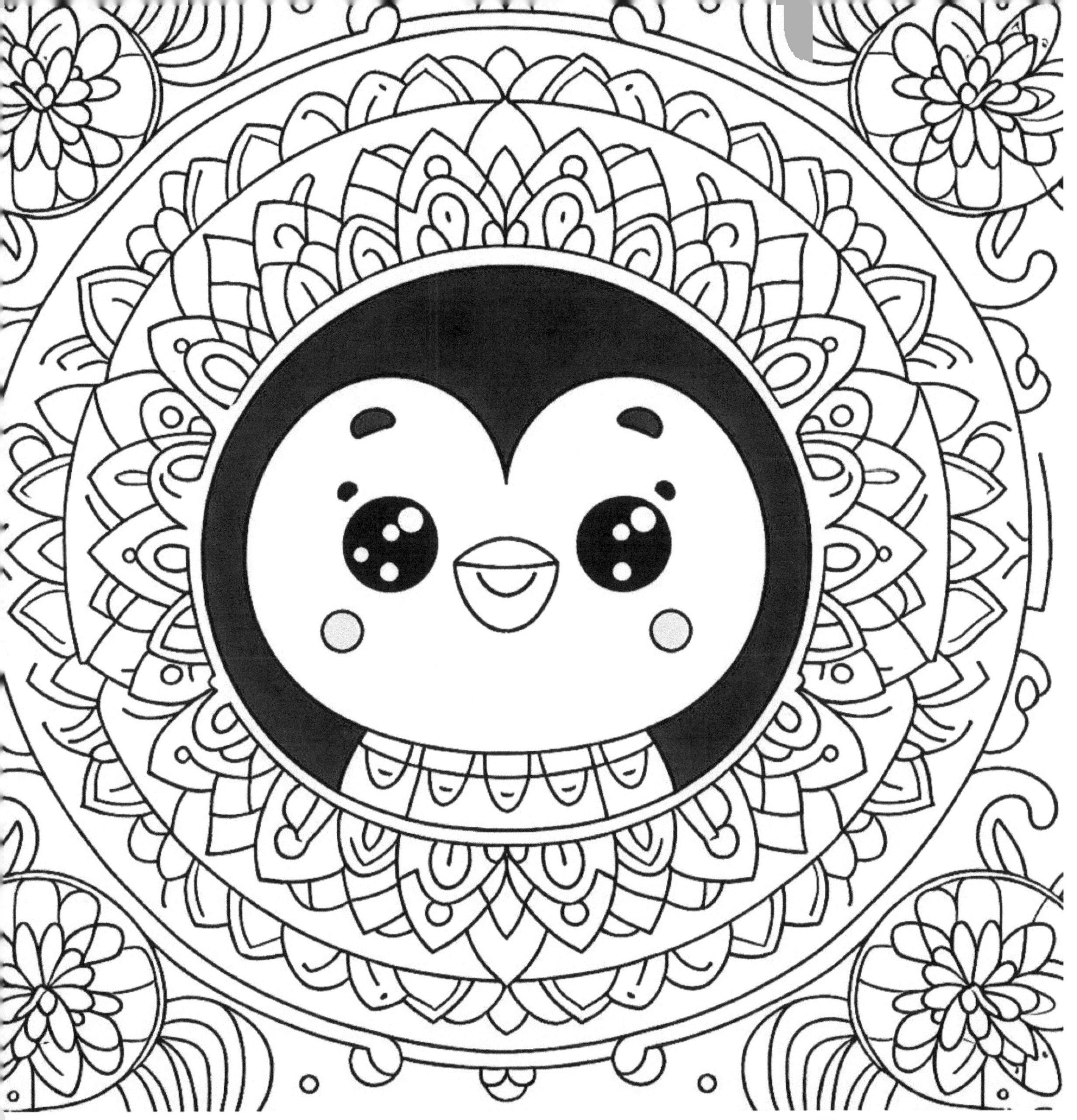

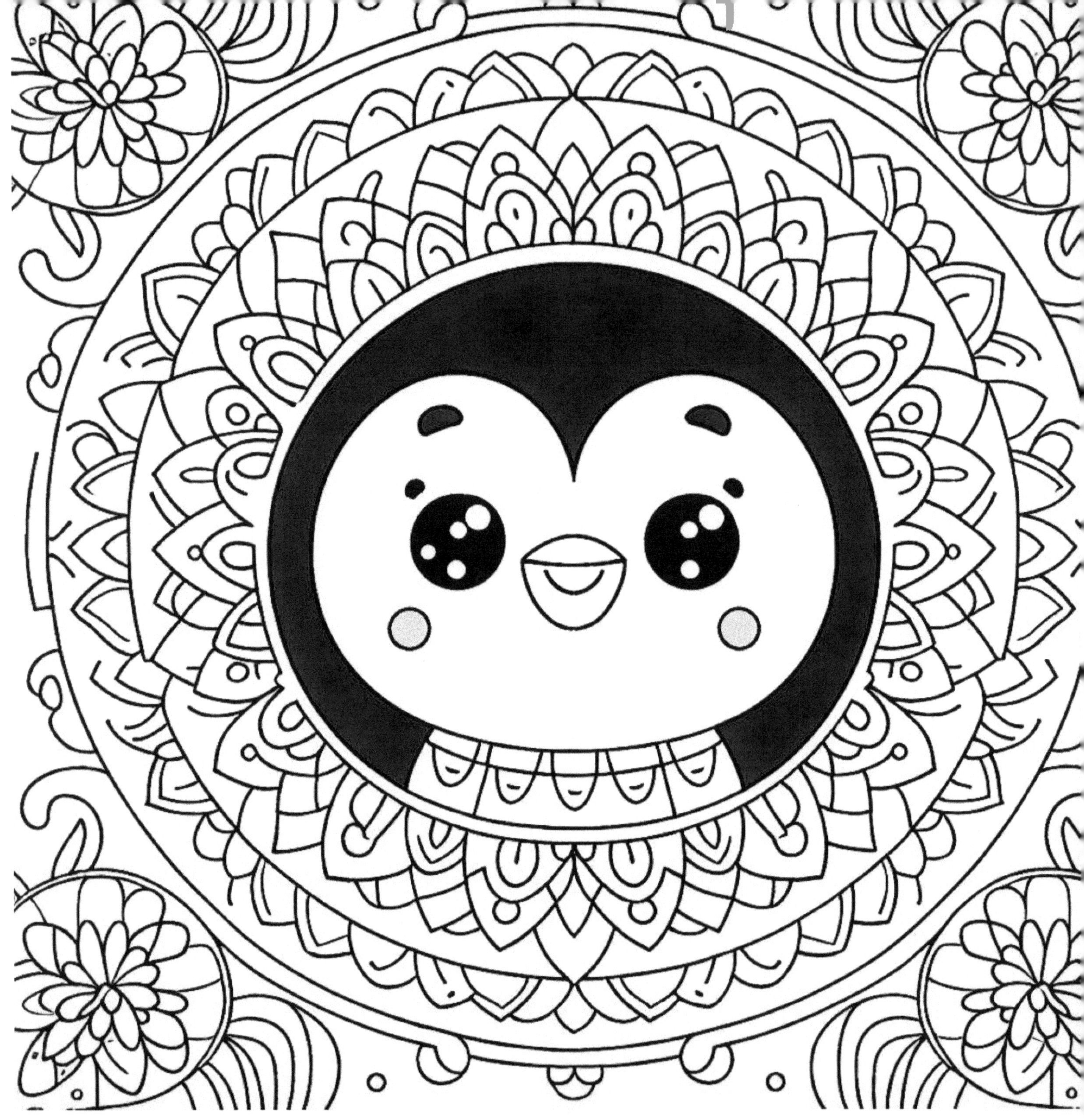

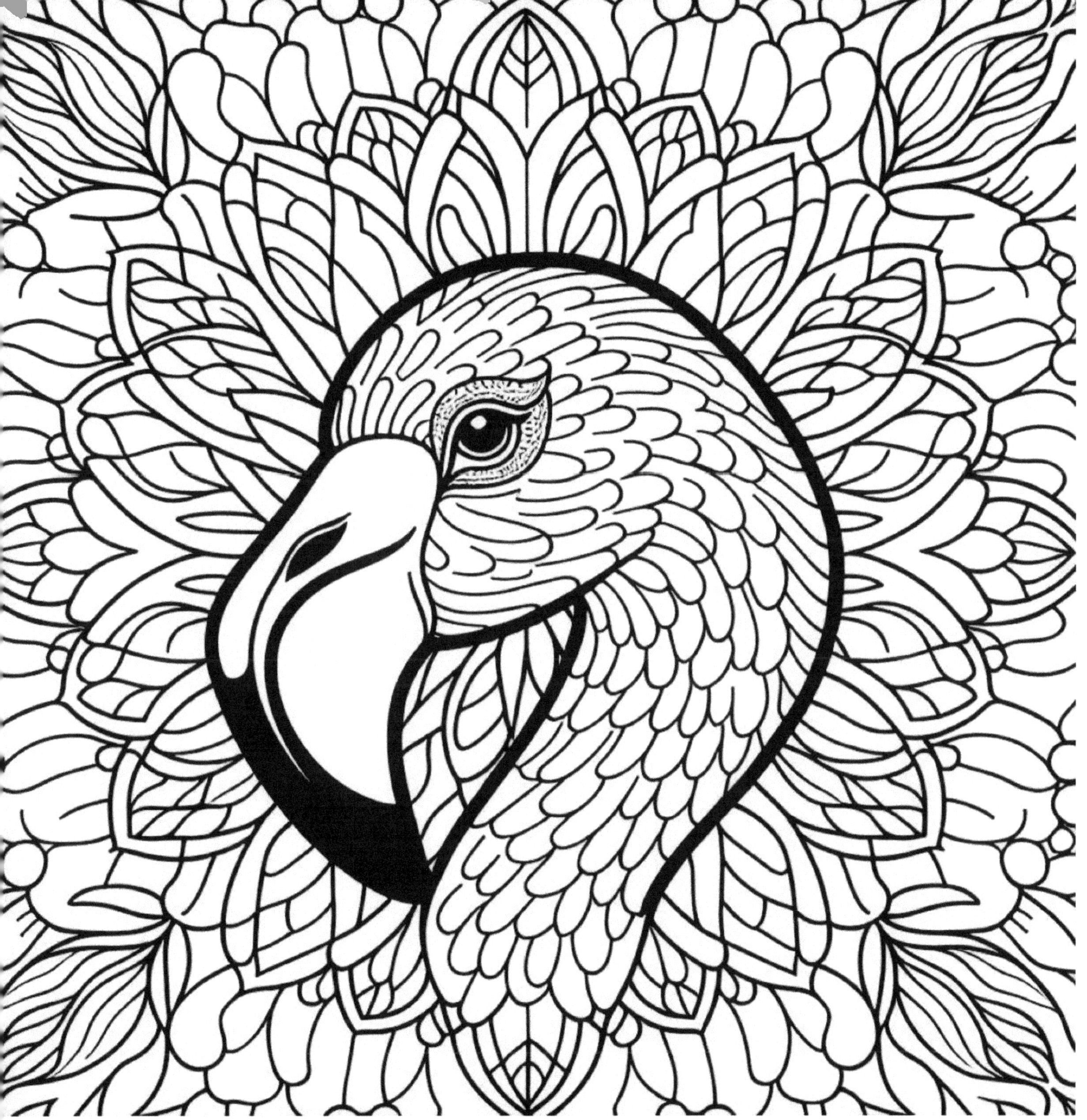

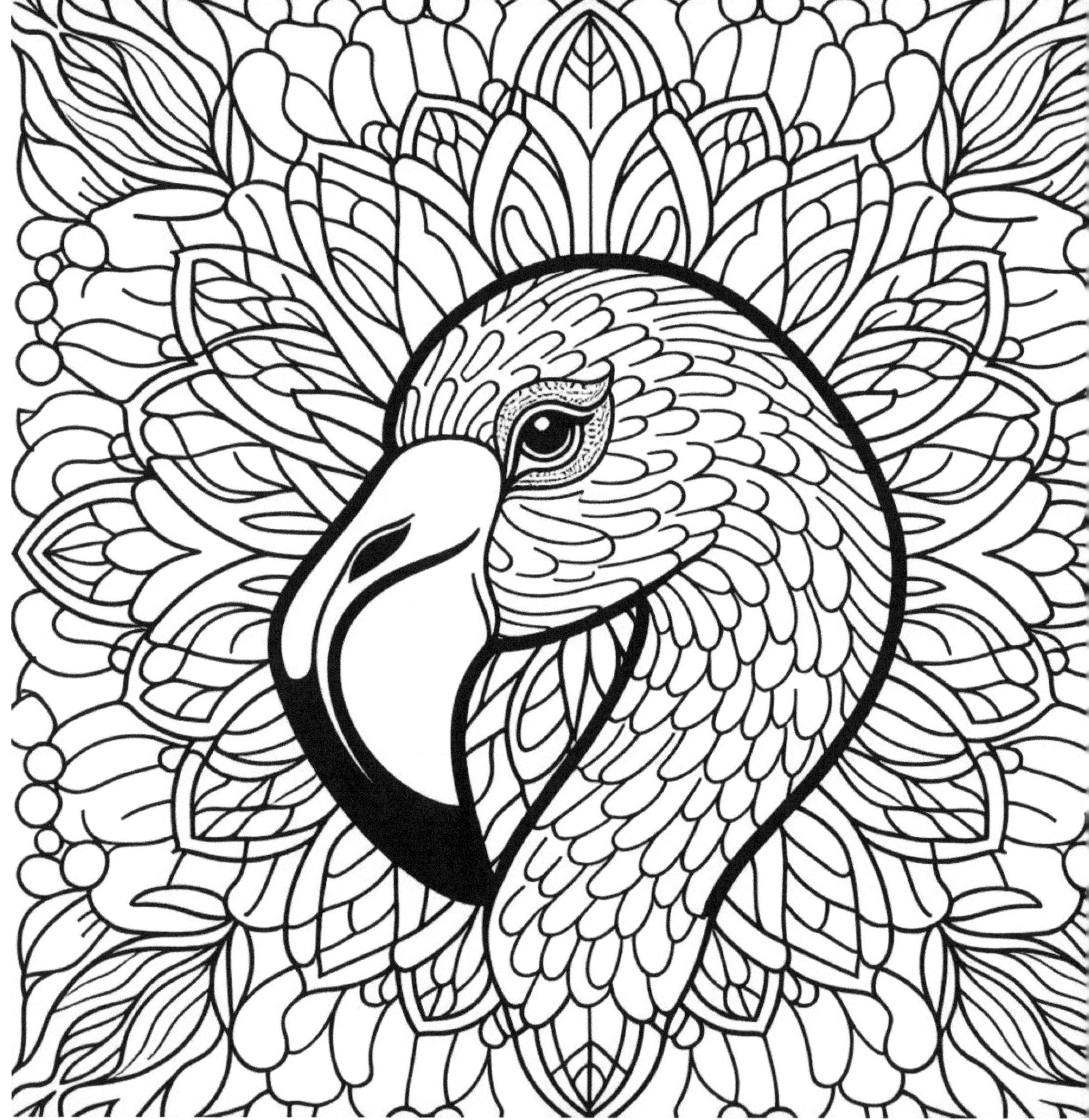

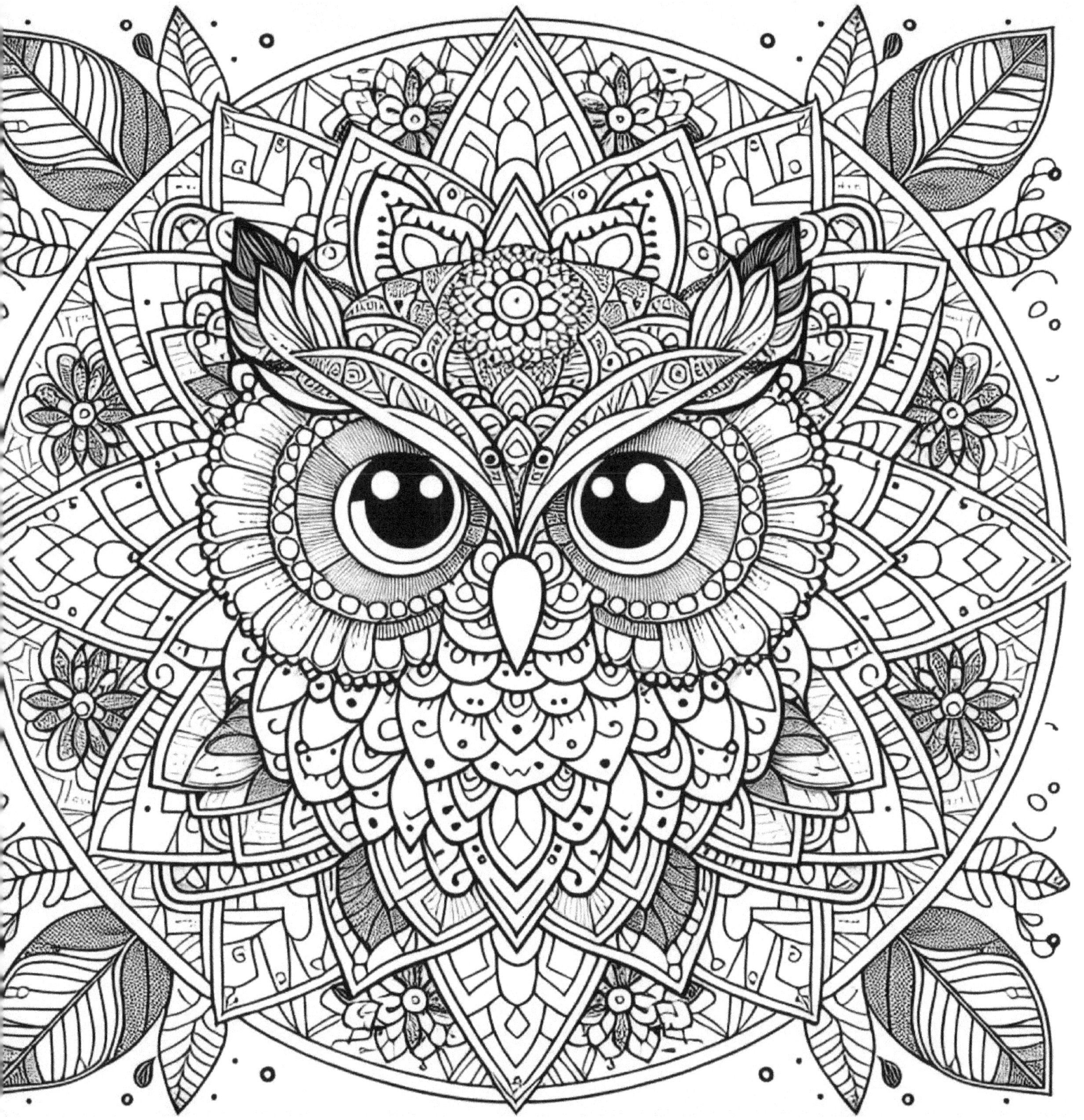

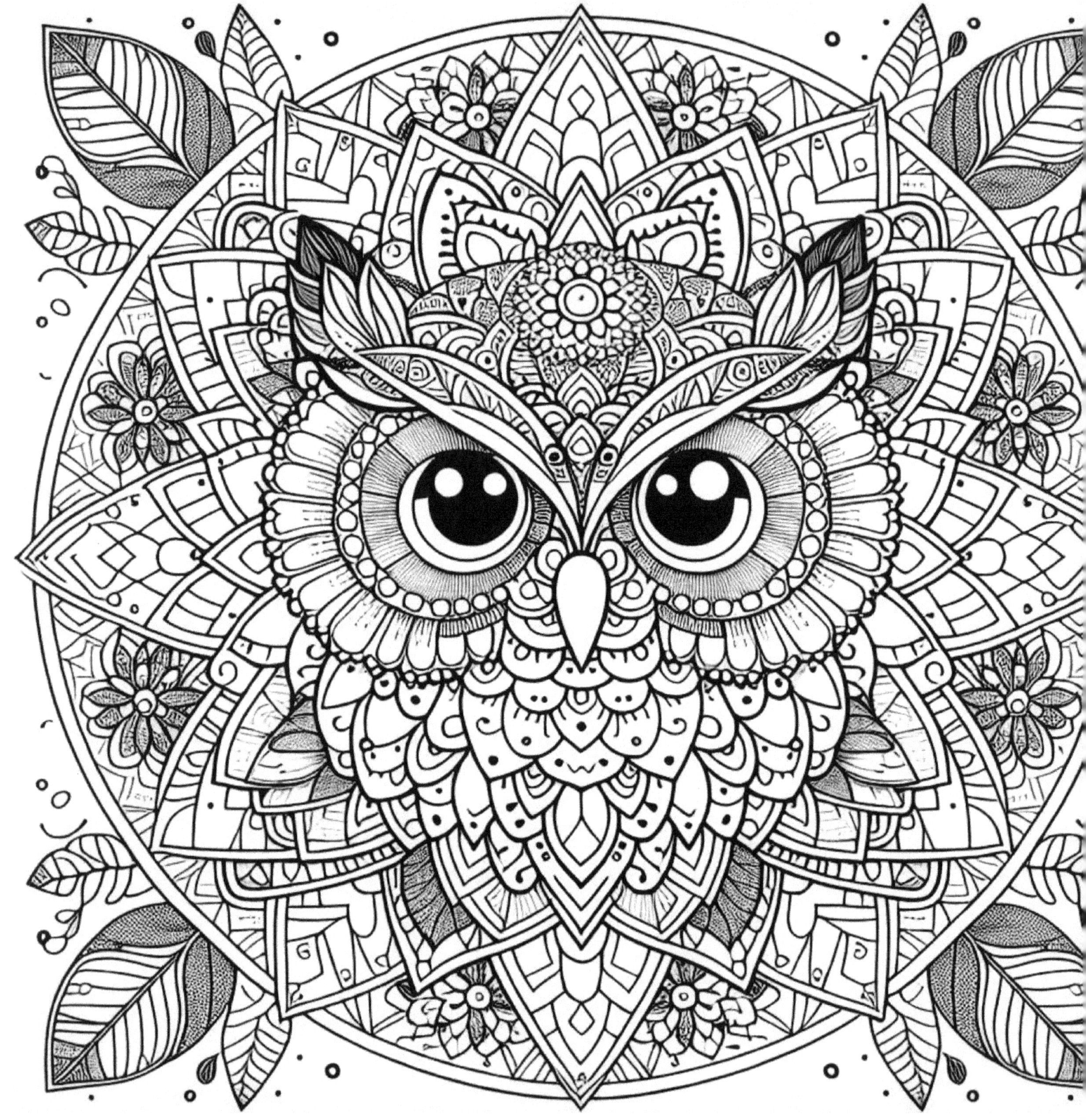

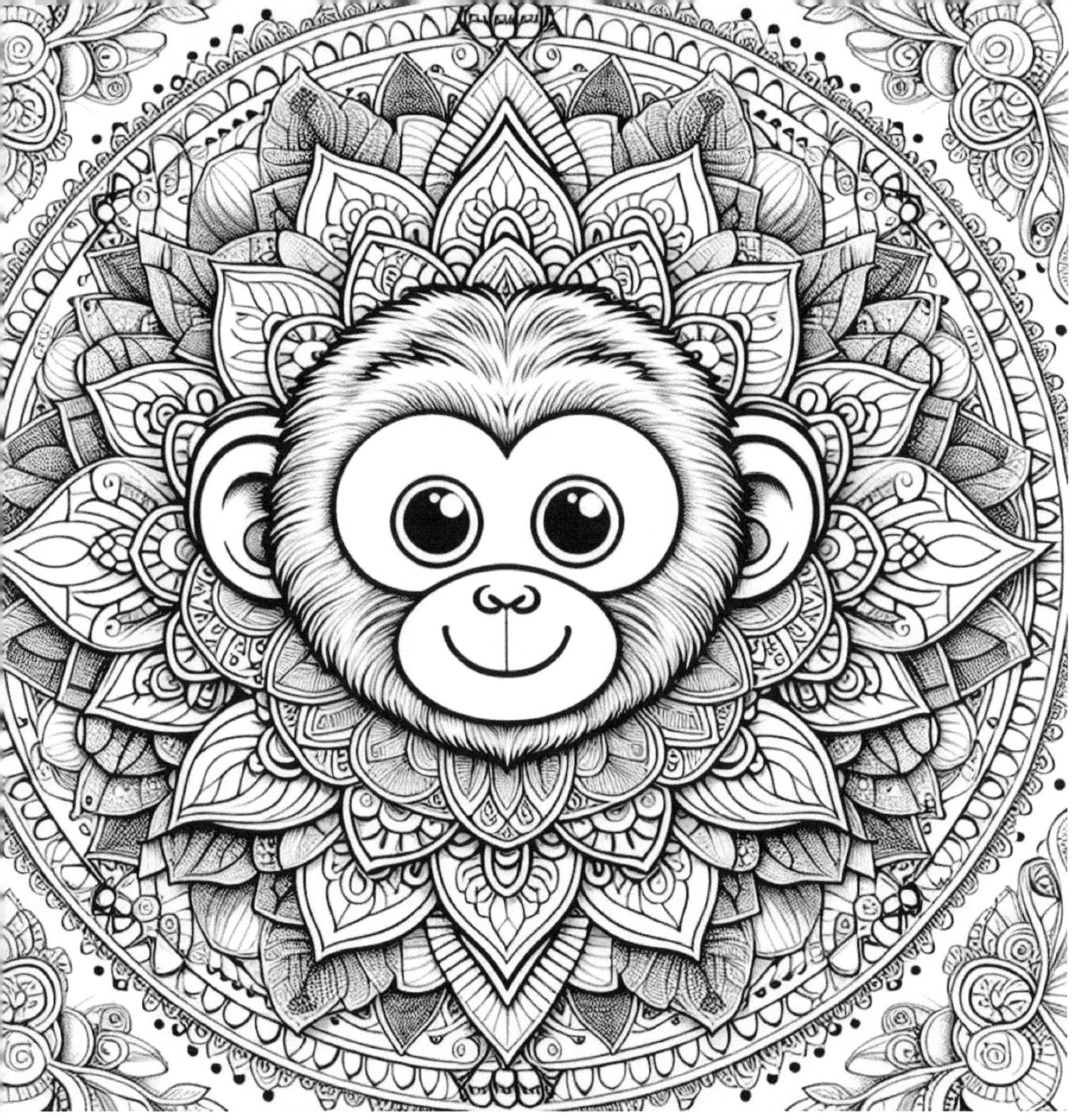

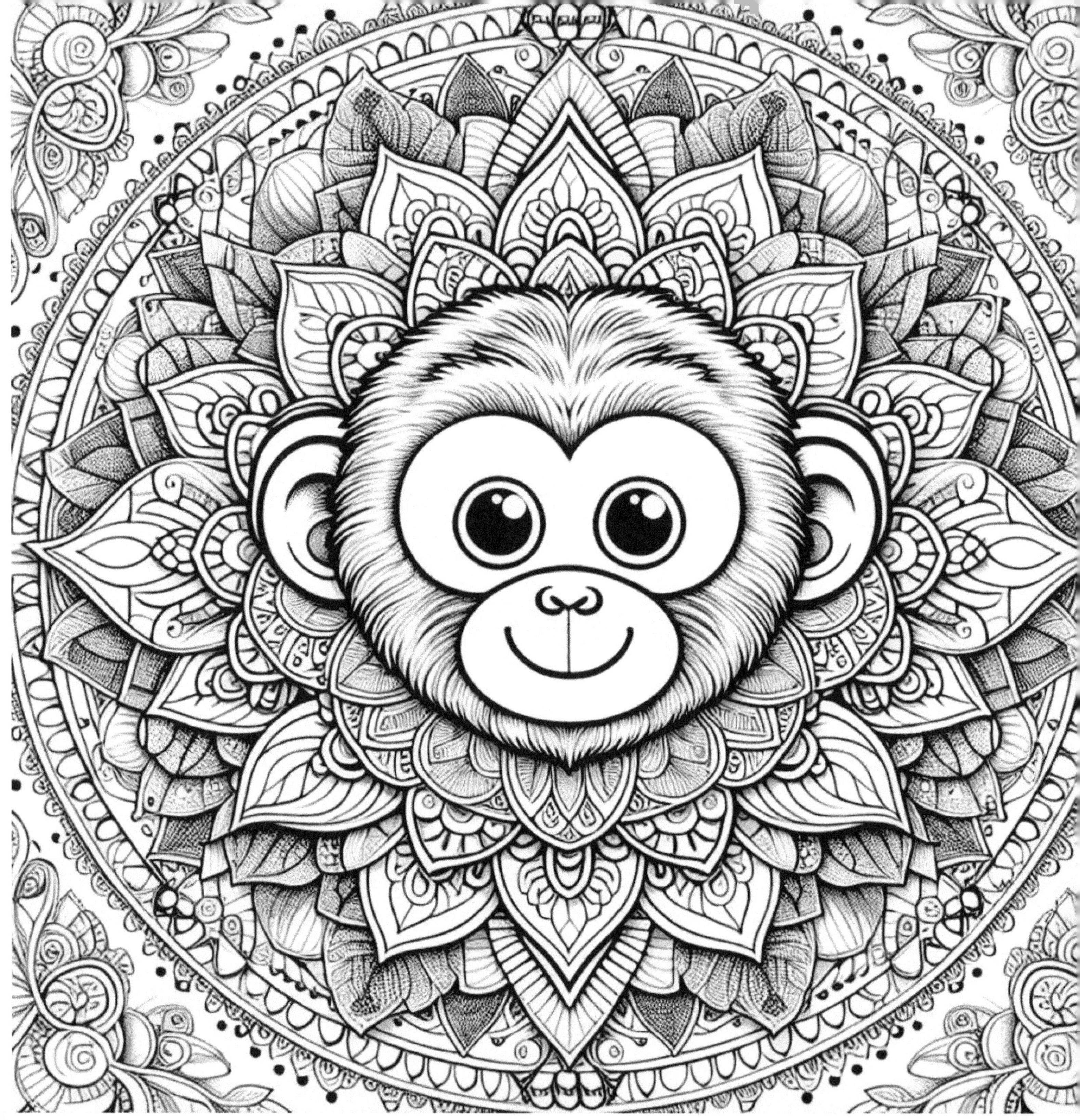

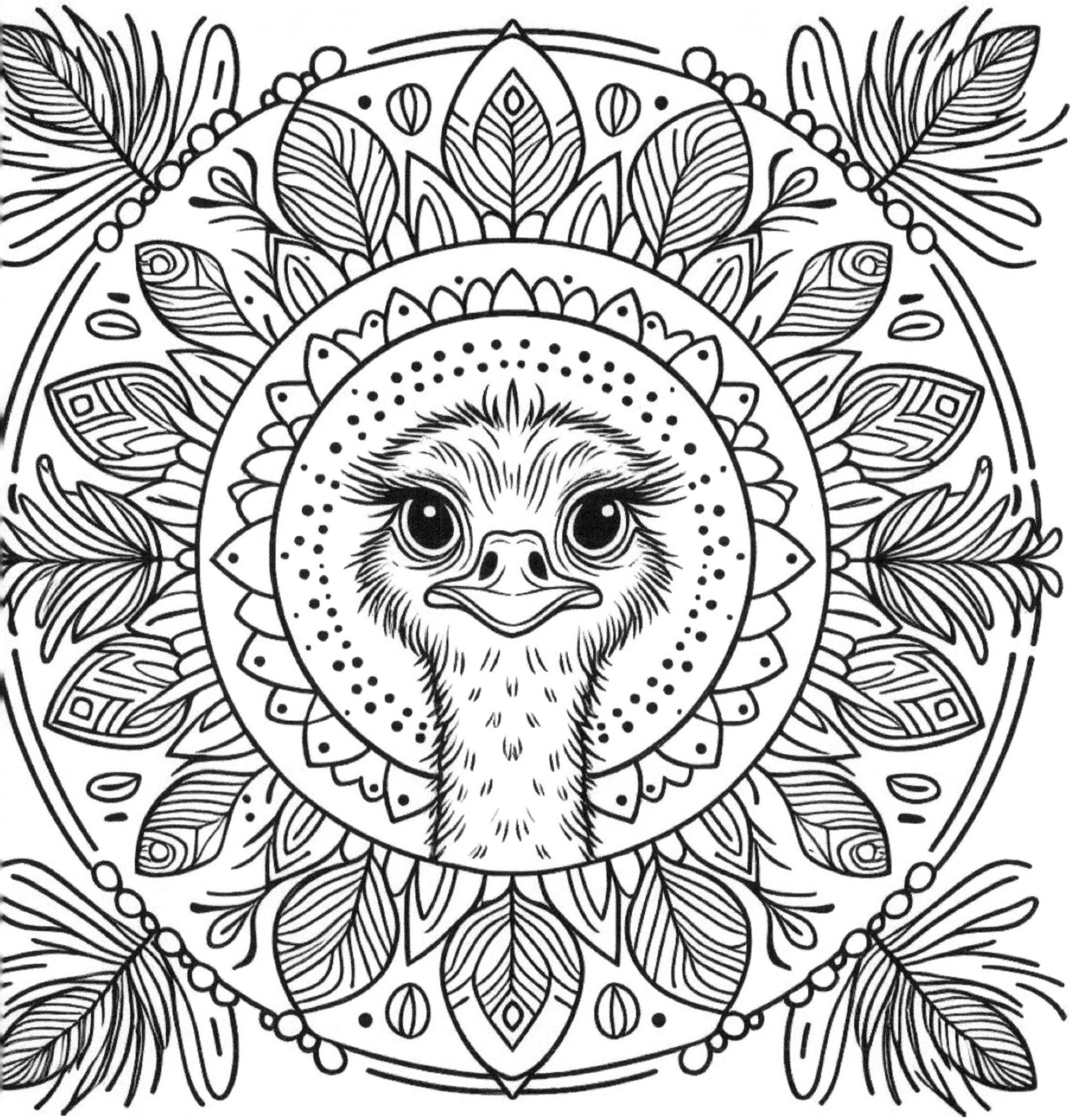

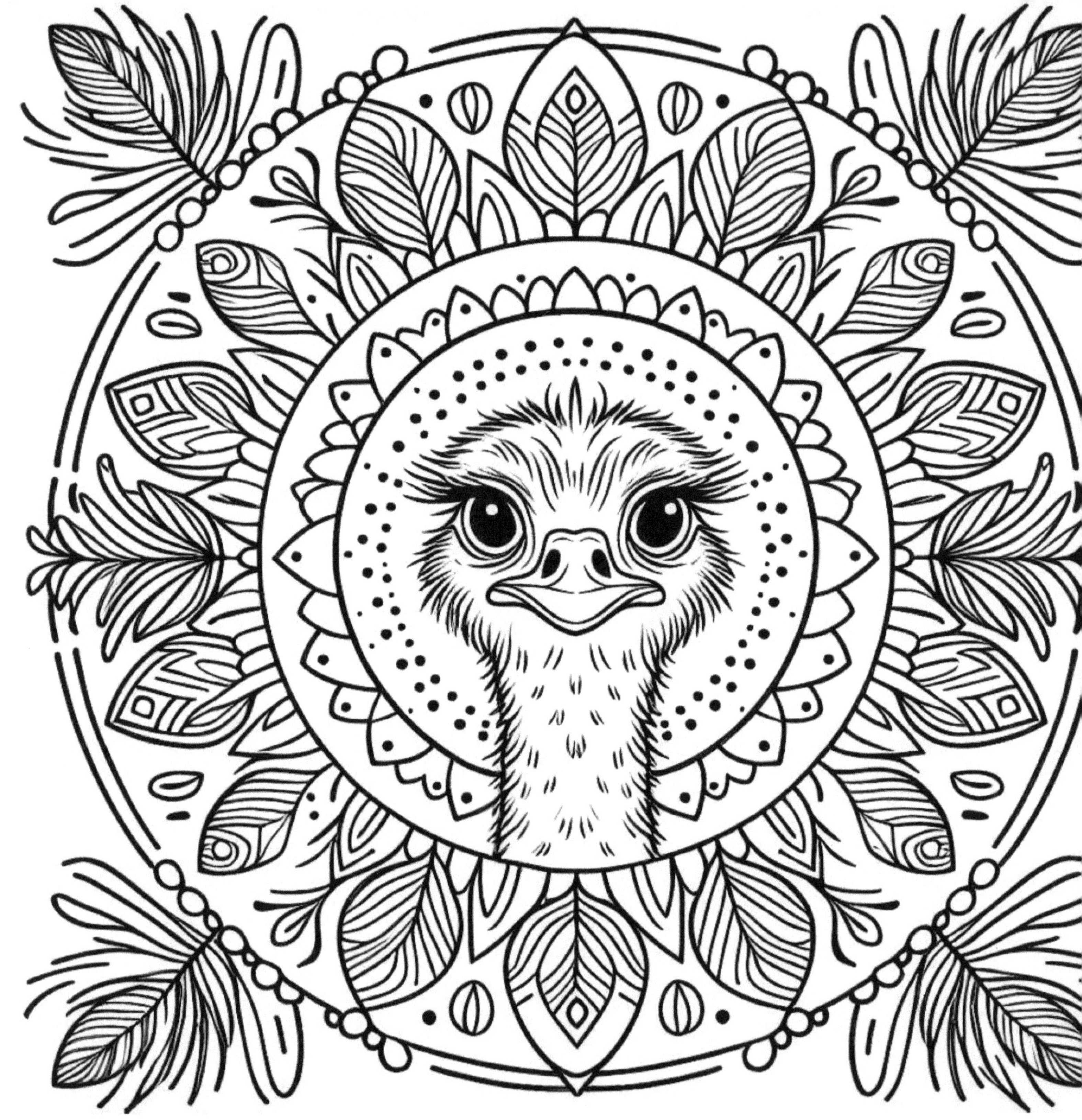

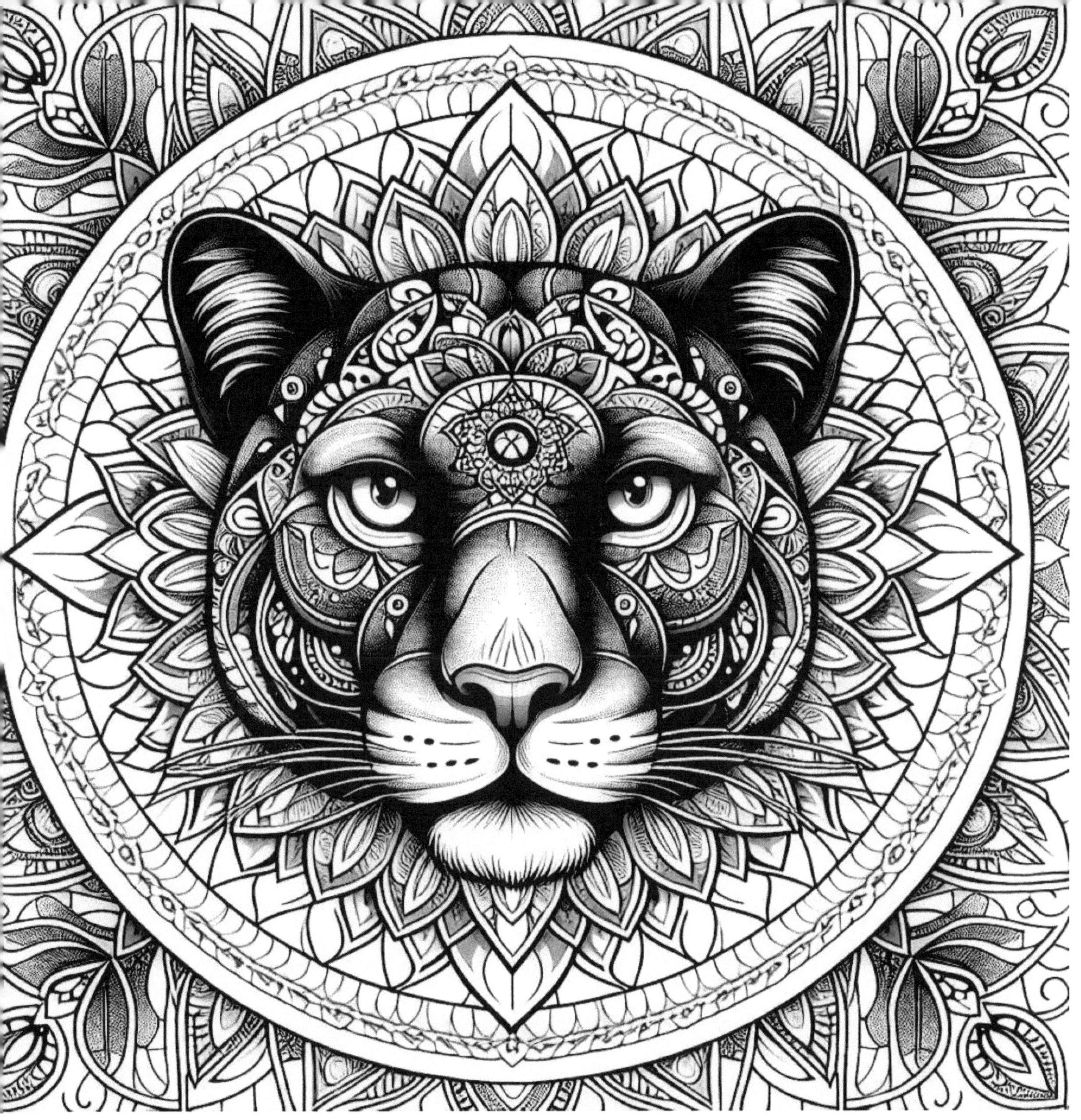

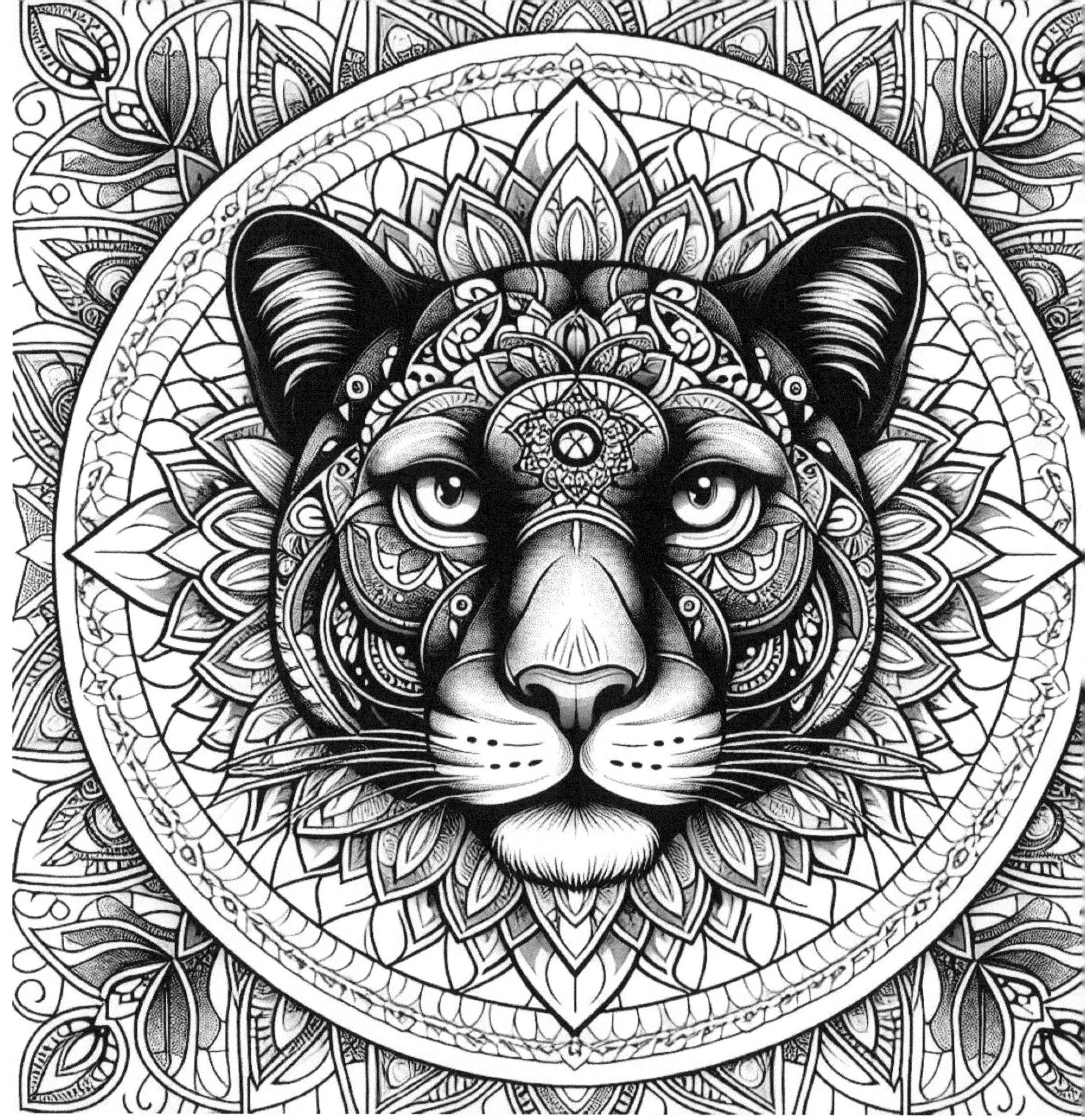

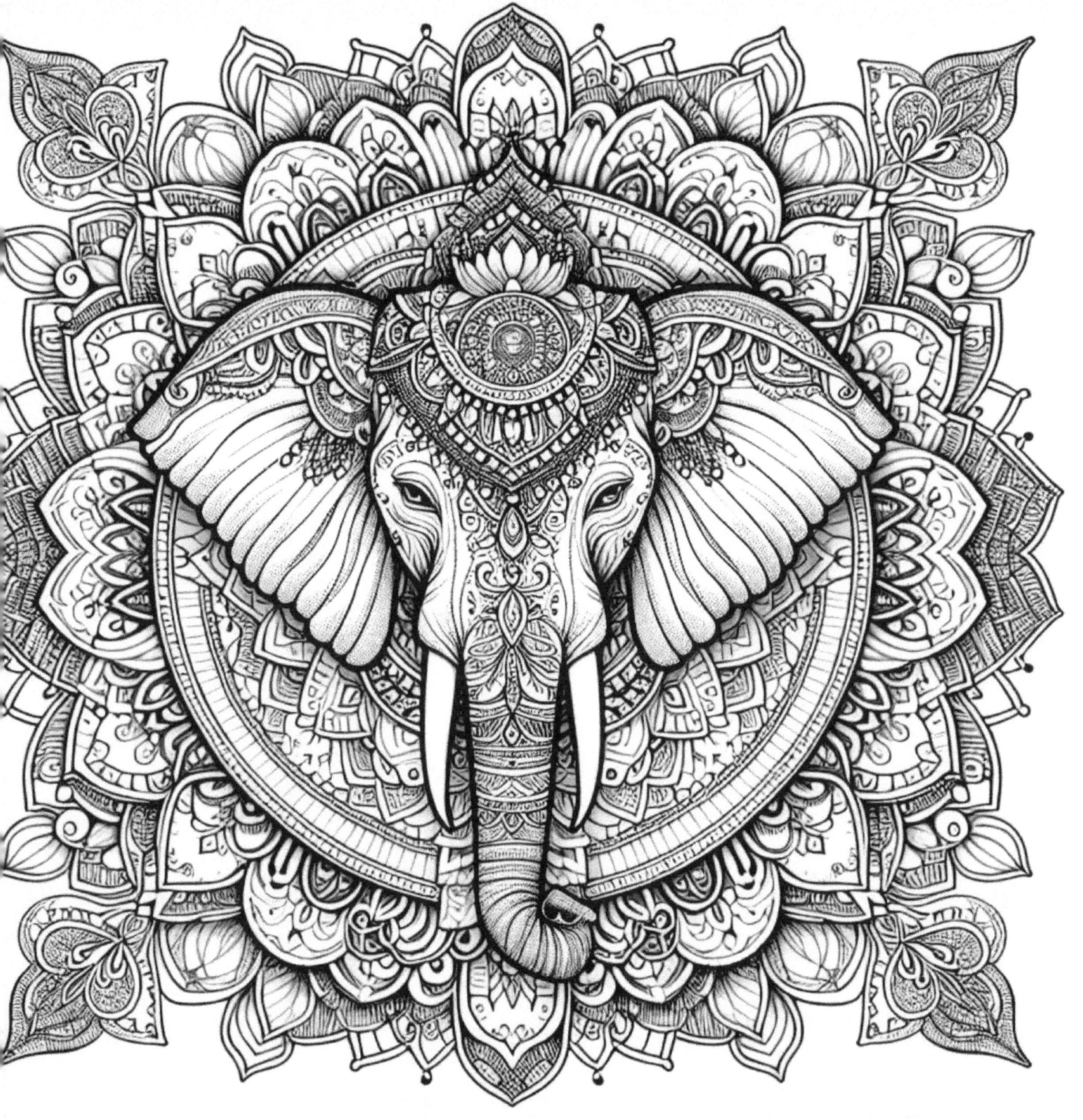

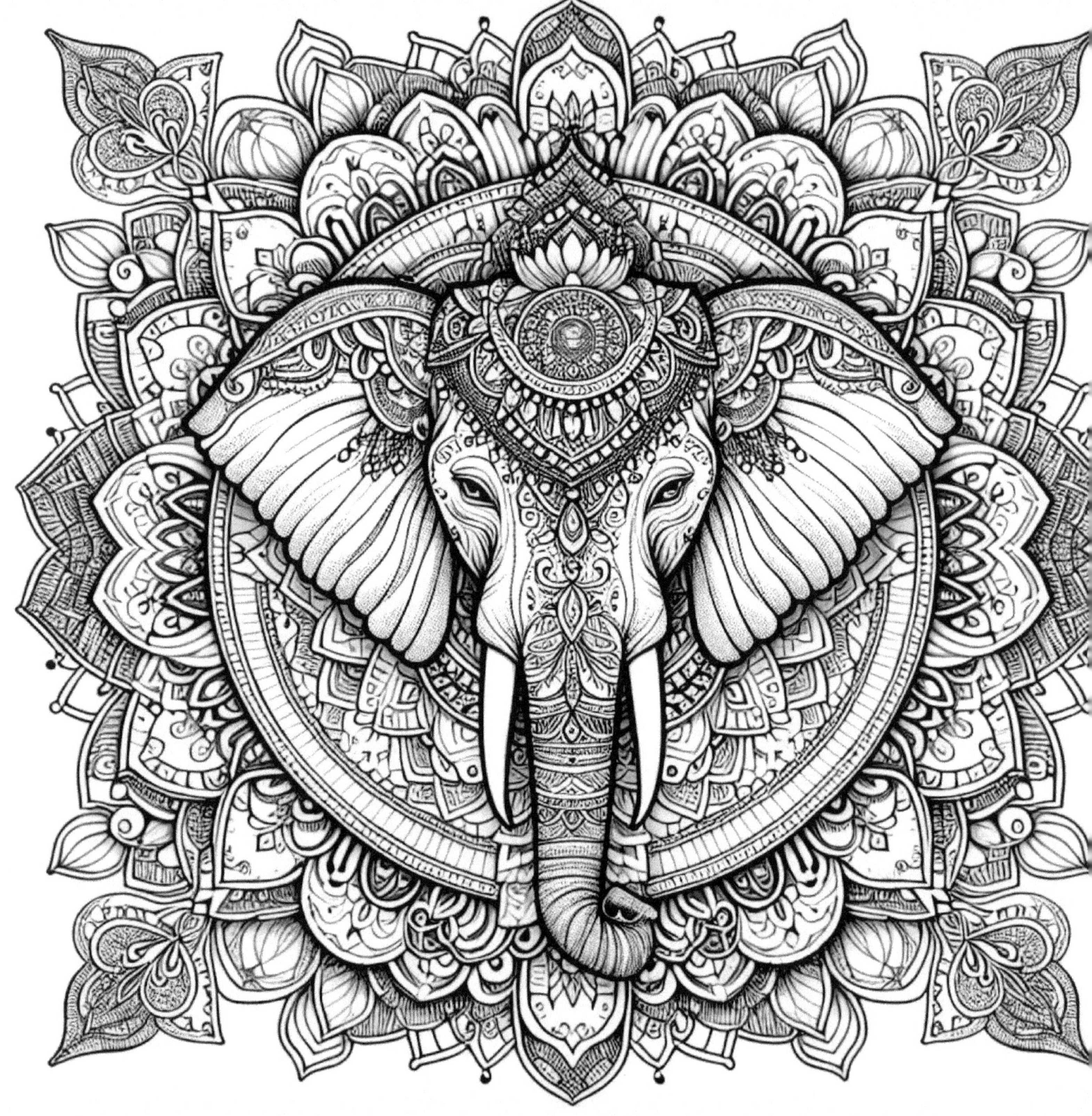

www.ingramcontent.com/pod-product-compliance
Lightning Source LLC
Chambersburg PA
CBHW040218110726
48005CB00019B/3071

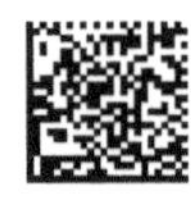
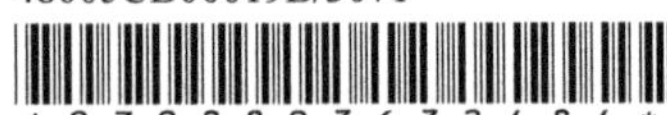